# INTRO TO CYBERSECURITY

A PRACTITIONER'S STUDY GUIDE

# INTRO TO CYBERSECURITY

## A PRACTITIONER'S STUDY GUIDE

**DAVID LEE EVENDEN**
Cybersecurity Analyst

**DOMINIC CARRERA**
Security Systems Engineer

Oversight: Kent Potter
Book Design: Loryn O'Donnell
Illustrations: Erin DeGroot
Content Contributors: Information Security Practitioners

ISBN-13: 978-1-7344107-2-3

Copyright © 2020 StandardUser Cyber Security. All rights reserved.

# FOREWORDS

There was a time when our vision of a technology professional was someone like the comic book store owner from The Simpsons. An overweight, white male who spent more time in his basement than in the sun; but times, well, *they are a changin'*.

Today, the barrier of entry for technology jobs is shifting greatly as the industry itself is changing drastically. Cybersecurity has not escaped this trend. When I stop and think of where my Cybersecurity analyst friends work, we have H.E.B (grocery store), Valero (petroleum refinery) and Starbucks Coffee. It's obvious there is no shortage of companies building Cybersecurity teams to keep their company safe. It's easy to see that more individuals will be needed to fill these roles. What is not so obvious is how we recruit and train them?

Getting started in the Cybersecurity industry has felt like one big cryptographic game. Often times, sentences like *"The ISSM sent the RMF package to the SCA via EMASS. There were a few CAT3 STIGs open in the SCC, but they got an ATO,"* may be used to communicate a point. Sentences like this—alphabet soup sentences as I like to call them—frequently feel like they are intended to keep out anyone new to the industry. Circumstances like this are why I started the "It's Okay to Be New" mantra.

The goal of "It's Okay to Be New" is to help foster a community where it's okay to ask for help. A community where it is okay to admit what we don't know, and most importantly, a community where it is okay to ask for training, education, and mentorship.

This is why I was so excited when David contacted me about his new book, "An Introduction to Cybersecurity". Having a resource that can be given to someone starting out in the industry, that breaks down concepts from APT and Wireshark analysis with no preconceived notions about what someone should already know, will be a valuable tool in growing our community.

Something that has significantly held me back throughout my career is the fear of not knowing enough - I hate the vulnerable feeling that comes with admitting that I don't know the answer, especially when it feels like an answer I should know. We all deal with this in our day-to-day lives, but it's a consistent problem in the technology field. When I first started as a Linux Administrator, I thought it was "cool" to drink from the firehose and overwhelm myself trying to learn everything, but over time I realized that doesn't scale well at all. This can feel extremely overwhelming when you're pivoting to Cybersecurity. Even if you come in with previous technology experience, it often feels like a whole new world. It's amazing, because you get to meet and talk to so many brilliant minds; however, it can be overwhelming, because you start to wonder where you fit within the community. This was heavy on my mind in the year leading up to my introduction to the Cybersecurity field. I couldn't figure out where to even start.

Ell Marquez
Community Architect

When Ell started the "It's Okay to Be New" movement, I knew it was important. We're constantly having community conversations on how to minimize gatekeeping, but it's hard to apply actionable steps that need to be taken to solve this problem.

I think the "It's Okay to Be New" movement is an amazing first step towards greater inclusion in cybersecurity. The concept of putting time aside to help build the community up by allowing others to come in is so important. It's incredibly refreshing to go to conferences to see a beginner track, where someone can comfortably dip their toes into the water by learning the fundamentals of the industry, rather than trying to dive into the deep end immediately, only to be potentially scared away by the overwhelming amount of in-depth technical conversations and presentations that are occurring.

Seniors in the field giving back to the community by spreading their knowledge is critical, and it's amazing to see. The more knowledge you gain, I challenge you to give back to the community what you can, even if you're still learning. It's so easy to look at everything going on in cybersecurity and suddenly feel like you don't know enough or you are not technical enough or you just don't belong. But when a person (or a group of people) takes the time to say, "You're new? It's okay! Break out your laptop, let me show you some stuff!" it completely alters that mindset.

When egos are shed and we work together and give back to the community as we delve deeper into it ourselves, amazing things happen. When David reached out and asked me to be part of this, I was ecstatic, because the foundations for this book align perfectly with the ideals of building a stronger community by helping others join in.

While you read this book, and throughout your cybersecurity journey - I highly encourage you to have an open mind, learn as much as you can, listen to as many people as you can, and when you're ready - give back to the community. I hope this book helps you dip your toes in the water and get an idea of where you'd like your path to lead you. You've got this!

Allie Barnes
Cloud Operations Engineer

# TABLE OF CONTENTS

| | |
|---|---|
| **THREAT MANAGEMENT** | 1 |
| ENVIRONMENTAL RECONNAISSANCE | 3 |
|     KNOWING & UNDERSTANDING YOUR ENVIRONMENT | 3 |
|     PROCEDURES, COMMON TASKS, & VARIABLES | 4 |
|     TOPOLOGY DISCOVERY | 4 |
|     OS FINGERPRINTING | 4 |
|     SERVICE DISCOVERY | 5 |
|     PACKET CAPTURE | 5 |
|     LOG REVIEW | 6 |
|     ROUTER / FIREWALL ACL REVIEW | 7 |
|     EMAIL HARVESTING | 7 |
|     SOCIAL ENGINEERING | 8 |
|     SOCIAL MEDIA PROFILING | 11 |
|     DNS HARVESTING | 11 |
|     TECHNOLOGICAL VARIABLES | 12 |
|     TOOLS | 13 |
|     PACKET ANALYZER | 15 |
|     IDS / IPS | 15 |
|     HIDS / NIDS | 16 |
|     FIREWALL RULE BASED & LOGS | 16 |
|     SYSLOG | 16 |
|     VULNERABILITY SCANNER | 17 |
| RECONNAISSANCE RESULTS | 18 |
|     POINT-IN-TIME & DATA CORRELATION / ANALYTICS | 18 |
|     PACKET, PROTOCAL, & TRAFFIC ANALYSIS | 18 |
|     NETFLOW ANALYSIS | 18 |
|     WIRELESS ANALYSIS | 18 |
|     DATA CORRELATION & ANALYTICS | 19 |
|     DATA OUTPUT TOOLS | 19 |

| | |
|---|---|
| SYSLOG & DIFFERENT TYPES OF LOGS | 19 |
| PACKET ANALYZERS & OUTPUT FROM PACKET CAPTURES | 22 |
| NMAP | 23 |
| IDS & IDS REPORT | 24 |
| NETWORK BASED THREAT MITIGATION | 27 |
| NETWORK SEGMENTATION | 27 |
| JUMP SERVER | 28 |
| NETWORK ACCESS CONTROL | 29 |
| HARDENING, HONEYPOTS, ENDPOINT SECURITY, & GROUP POLICIES | 31 |
| MANDATORY ACCESS CONTROL (MAC) | 31 |
| COMPENSATING CONTROLS | 31 |
| BLOCKING UNUSED PORTS / SERVICES | 31 |
| PATCHING | 31 |
| HONEYPOT | 31 |
| END POINT SECURITY | 32 |
| CORPORATE SECURITY BEST PRACTICES | 33 |
| PENETRATION TESTING | 33 |
| TRAINING & EXERCISES | 35 |
| REVERSE ENGINEERING | 35 |
| SANDBOXING | 35 |
| REVERSE ENGINEERING HARDWARE | 36 |
| THE CIA TRIAD | 36 |
| TYPES OF THREATS | 38 |
| RISK | 39 |
| RISK EVALUATION | 39 |
| ASSESSING RISK | 40 |
| MANAGING RISK | 41 |
| NON-TECHNICAL SOURCES OF RISK | 42 |
| **VULNERABILITY MANAGEMENT: PROCESSES & SCANNING** | **45** |
| INFORMATION SECURITY VULNERABILITY MANAGEMENT PROCESS | 47 |
| REGULATORY ENVIRONEMENTS | 47 |
| CORPORATE POLICY | 48 |
| DATA CLASSIFICATION | 49 |

| | |
|---|---|
| ESTABLISH SCANNING FREQUENCY | 49 |
| FURTHER CONFIGURATIONS OF VULNERABILITY SCANNERS | 50 |
| SCANNING CRITERIA & SENSITIVITY LEVELS | 50 |
| VULNERABILITY FEED | 50 |
| SCOPE | 50 |
| CREDENTIALED VS. NON-CREDENTIALED | 51 |
| SERVER-BASED VS. AGENT-BASED | 51 |
| TOOL UPDATES / PLUG-INS | 51 |
| SCAP | 51 |
| GENERATING REPORTS | 52 |
| TYPES OF FINDINGS | 52 |
| REMEDIATION | 53 |
| ANALYZING VULNERABILITY SCANS: REPORTS | 55 |
| ANALYZING REPORTS | 55 |
| FALSE POSITIVES & EXCEPTIONS | 58 |
| ANALYZING VULNERABILITY SCANS: CORRELATION | 59 |
| RELATED LOGS & RECONCILING RESULTS | 59 |
| DETERMINE TRENDS | 59 |
| BEST PRACTICES | 60 |
| **VULNERABILITY MANAGEMENT: COMMON VULNERABILITIES** | **63** |
| SERVERS & ENDPOINTS | 65 |
| MISSING PATCHES | 65 |
| BUFFER OVERFLOWS | 66 |
| ARBITRARY CODE EXECUTION | 66 |
| INSECURE PROTOCAL USE | 66 |
| SQL INJECTION | 67 |
| TYPES OF SQLI ATTACKS | 67 |
| XSS | 68 |
| VIRTUAL INFRASTRUCTURE | 68 |
| VIRTUAL HOSTS | 68 |
| VIRTUAL NETWORKS | 69 |
| VIRTUAL INFRASTRUCTURE MANAGEMENT INTERFACE | 69 |
| NETWORK APPLIANCES & INFRASTRUCTURE | 69 |

| | |
|---|---|
| MOBILE & INTERCONNECTED NETWORKS | 70 |
|     MOBILE DEVICES | 70 |
|     INTERCONNECTED NETWORKS | 70 |
| VPNs, ISCs, & SCADA | 72 |
|     VPNS | 72 |
|     ISCs & SCADA | 73 |
| **CYBER INCIDENT RESPONSE** | **75** |
| THREAT CLASSIFICATION | 77 |
|     KNOWN VS. UNKNOWN | 78 |
|     ZERO DAY | 78 |
|     ADVANCED PERSISTENT THREAT | 79 |
| FACTORS OF DETERMINATION | 80 |
|     INCIDENT SEVERITY & PRIORITIZATION | 80 |
|     DATA INTEGRITY | 80 |
|     TYPES OF DATA | 81 |
| COMMON SYMPTOMS | 82 |
|     NETWORK RELATED | 82 |
|     APPLICATION RELATED | 84 |
|     HOST RELATED | 85 |
| DETERMINING INCIDENT IMPACT | 87 |
|     SCOPE OF IMPACT | 87 |
|     DOWNTIME | 87 |
|     SYSTEM PROCESS CRITICALITY | 87 |
|     RECOVERY TIME | 87 |
|     DATA RECOVERY | 88 |
|     ECONOMIC | 88 |
| FORENSICS TOOLKIT | 89 |
|     DIGITAL FORENSICS WORKSTATION | 89 |
|     WRITE BLOCKERS | 89 |
|     CABLES & DRIVE ADAPTERS | 89 |
|     WIPED REMOVABLE MEDIA | 89 |
|     CAMERAS | 89 |
|     CRIME TAPE | 90 |

| | |
|---|---|
| TAMPER-PROOF SEALS | 90 |
| DOCUMENTATION / FORMS | 90 |
| ESSENTIALS OF COMMUNICATION | 91 |
| STAKEHOLDERS | 92 |
| PURPOSE OF COMMUNICATION PROCESSES | 93 |
| ROLE-BASED RESPONSIBILITIES | 93 |
| RETAIN INCIDENT RESPONSE PROVIDER | 94 |
| INCIDENT SYMPTOMS & RECOVERY | 95 |
| CONTAINMENT TECHNIQUES | 95 |
| ERADICATION TECHNIQUES | 97 |
| VALIDATION | 98 |
| CORRECTIVE ACTIONS | 99 |
| INCIDENT SUMMARY REPORT | 99 |
| **RELATIONAL SECURITY PRACTICES** | **101** |
| REGULATORY COMPLIANCE | 103 |
| FRAMEWORKS & CONTROLS | 105 |
| POLICIES & PROCEDURES | 107 |
| VERIFICATION & QUALITY CONTROL | 109 |
| **SECURITY OF IDENTITY & ACCESS MANAGEMENT** | **113** |
| CONTEXT-BASED AUTHENTICATION | 115 |
| TIME | 115 |
| LOCATION | 115 |
| BEHAVIORAL | 115 |
| IDENTITIES & IDENTITY REPOSITORIES | 116 |
| ISSUES ASSOCIATED WITH IDENTITIES | 116 |
| ISSUES ASSOCIATED WITH IDENTITY REPOSITORIES | 116 |
| FEDERATION AUTHENTICATION & SINGLE SIGN-ON | 120 |
| SECURITY ISSUES | 120 |
| EXPLOITS | 121 |
| IMPERSONATION | 121 |
| MAN-IN-THE-MIDDLE | 121 |
| SESSION HIJACK | 121 |
| CROSS-SITE SCRIPTING | 122 |

| | |
|---|---|
| PRIVILEGE ESCALATION | 123 |
| ROOTKIT | 123 |
| **COMPENSATING CONTROLS & SECURE CODING** | **125** |
| SECURITY ANALYTICS & MANUAL REVIEW | 127 |
|     SECURITY DATA ANALYTICS | 127 |
|     TREND ANALYSIS | 127 |
|     HISTORICAL ANALYSIS | 127 |
|     MANUAL REVIEW | 128 |
| DEFENSE IN DEPTH | 129 |
|     PERSONNEL | 129 |
|     PROCESSES | 131 |
|     TECHNOLOGIES | 131 |
|     OTHER SECURITY CONCEPTS | 132 |
| SOFTWARE DEVELOPMENT BEST PRATICES | 133 |
|     MANUAL PEER REVIEW | 133 |
|     USER ACCEPTANCE TESTING | 134 |
|     STRESS TEST APPLICATION | 134 |
|     SECURITY REGRESSION TESTING | 134 |
| SECURE CODING BEST PRACTICES | 135 |
| **TOOLS & TECHNOLOGIES** | **137** |
| PREVENTIVE & COLLECTIVE TOOLS | 139 |
|     IDS & IPS | 139 |
|     HIPS | 139 |
|     FIREWALL | 139 |
|     ANTIVIRUS & ANTI-MALWARE | 140 |
|     DATA LOSS PREVENTION | 140 |
|     EMET | 140 |
|     WEB PROXY | 140 |
|     WEB APPLICATION FIREWALL | 141 |
|     SIEM | 141 |
|     NETWORK SCANNING | 142 |
|     VULNERABILITY SCANNING | 142 |
|     PACKET CAPTURE | 142 |

| | |
|---|---|
| COMMAND LINE / IP UTILITIES | 143 |
| ANALYTICAL TOOLS | 144 |
|     VULNERABILITY SCANNING | 144 |
|     SECURITY ANALYZER | 145 |
|     INTERCEPTION PROXY | 145 |
| EXPLOITATION TOOL SETS | 146 |
|     FRAMEWORK | 146 |
|     FUZZERS | 146 |
| FORENSIC TOOLKITS | 147 |
|     FORENSIC SUITES | 147 |
|     HASHING | 147 |
|     PASSWORD CRACKING | 147 |
|     IMAGING | 147 |
| NOTES | 149 |
| GLOSSARY | 157 |

# THREAT MANAGEMENT

# ENVIRONMENTAL RECONNAISSANCE

## KNOWING & UNDERSTANDING YOUR ENVIRONMENT

When conducting reconnaissance of a network, it is important to ask your customer for a baseline of the network. Remember that you are entering an environment which could already be compromised.

A baseline is the network's standard based on requirements and needs of the customer in order to deliver their product. Knowing what is supposed to be "normal" enables you, the analyst, to determine what is not normal and helps with identifying any false positives.

An example of this is a customer having telnet open. We know it is insecure, but the customer may have a reason to leave it open. This way, you know how to approach and assess the vulnerability.

It is also important to establish your baseline as an analyst. Running simple built-in commands, provides you with information from the perspective of the machine.

Sometimes establishing a baseline, prior to using tools, can help you identify a compromised host. When an attacker installs a rootkit, the binaries of the machine will provide misinformation, hiding the attacker's fingerprints.

Remember that as an analyst, your job is to be able to identify the minutest detail which can lead to an accurate assessment of the network. Knowing your environment before entering is the key to identifying those small clues.

## PROCEDURES, COMMON TASKS, & VARIABLES

Familiarizing yourself with common procedures and tasks related to cybersecurity is essential to understanding cybersecurity analysis. The following section will introduce you to procedures and variables that will influence how you approach situations as a security professional.

## TOPOLOGY DISCOVERY

Foremost in the process of identifying vulnerabilities, or securing a network, is discovering a network's topology. It would be difficult to secure a network without knowing what endpoints are in the network, and how those endpoints are arranged. A network's topology is simply how the communication devices are laid out that form the network. There are a few different topologies commonly used: star, ring, bus, mesh, point to point, and hybrid.

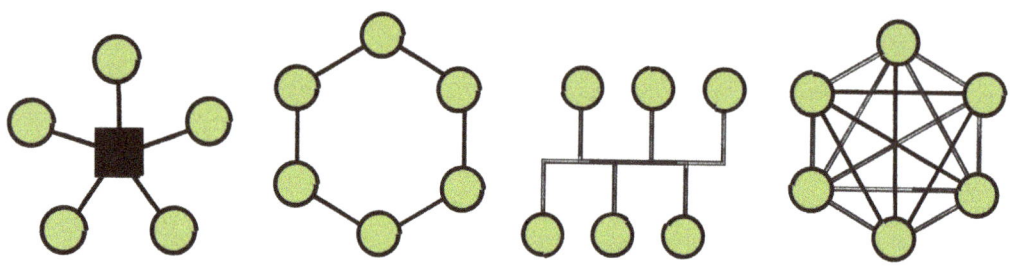

A powerful tool that can aid in the discovery of network endpoints and thus topology design is NMAP. NMAP is an open source network and host scanning tool, which can allow users to collect useful information and map a network.

## OS FINGERPRINTING

OS Fingerprinting seeks to determine the operating system of a host via context clues. This is often accomplished by tools that observe and analyze packets generated by the target host.

"Active Fingerprinting" tools like NMAP induce network traffic by sending packets to the target host and then analyzing the corresponding packets sent in reply. "Passive Fingerprinting" tools like NetworkMiner or P0f do not send packets to the target host. Instead, they collect & observe existing network traffic to analyze packets to and from the target host.

## SERVICE DISCOVERY

Since services generally correspond to specific ports, one method for discovering which services might be available on a host is to identify which ports are open on the target. For example, if a machine in a network has port 80 open, then they may be hosting an HTTP service.

NMAP can identify hosts on the network, enumerate open ports, and validate services running on those ports by interacting with them and seeing how they respond (fingerprinting), providing you with an overview of active endpoints, open ports, and validated services running on the network.

## PACKET CAPTURE

Packet capturing is the practice of collecting packets. A security professional might capture packets in order to analyze them with Wireshark, tcpdump, or another packet sniffing tool.

Wireshark allows you to both capture and analyze packets locally on a given host. Once you select the network interface from which you want to capture packets, Wireshark will reassemble, decode, colorize, and analyze those captured packets.

Capturing network traffic outside of your computer requires a device that has visibility into packets flowing across the network. This can include switches, routers, firewalls, or dedicated packet capturing appliances.

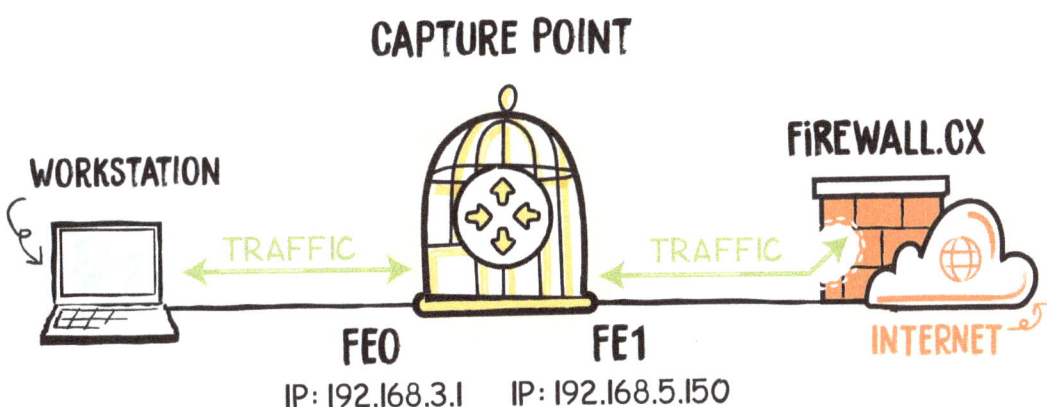

## LOG REVIEW

A log is a record of an event that has occurred on a particular machine or within a network. These records could include what traffic has been passed and what requests have been denied. Workstations, laptops, firewalls, routers, and many other devices create logs. Different devices can potentially produce different logs, though a common standard which provides consistency across devices is Syslog. The typical components of a log message include: timestamp, device identifier, message identifier, severity, and the event. These logs can be viewed on the device locally, or they can be aggregated onto a log server, or SIEM (discussed later). A log server, such as Graylog, provides a single place where logs can be collected for review. They also allow for automated notifications which are sent to administrators whenever important events occur.

Review these logs periodically to scrutinize what traffic has been on the network.

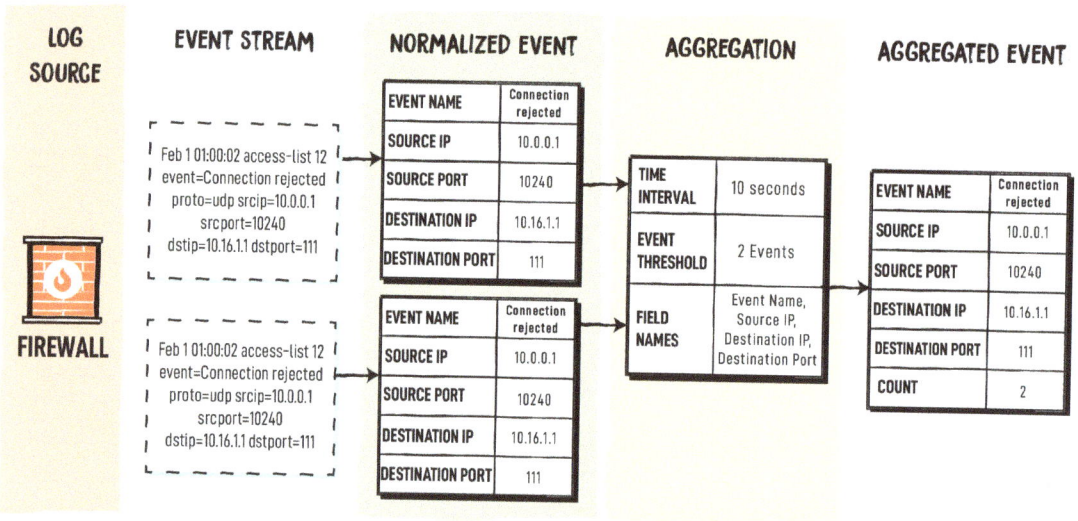

**HOW EVENT AGGREGATION WORKS**

# ROUTER / FIREWALL ACL REVIEW

Access control lists (ACL) are how firewalls and routers know whether or not traffic is appropriate to send to a certain node. Typically, they are analyzed in top-down order and use the first matching rule. Here is an example of an ACL:

| RULE | ACTION | DESTINATION IP | SOURCE IP | SOURCE PORT | DESTINATION PORT |
|------|--------|----------------|-----------|-------------|------------------|
| 1 | allow | any | 192.168.0.1 | any | 80 |
| 2 | deny | any | 192.168.0.1 | any | 25 |
| 3 | deny | 10.10.10.11 | any | any | any |
| 4 | deny | any | any | any | any |

Above, the "Action" column determines what the firewall should do in each situation. For rule 1, the firewall is told to allow any connection from the IP address 192.168.0.1 to port 80, which is often used for HTTP. So based on the above rules, any network traffic on port 80 that is sent by 192.168.0.1 through the firewall will be allowed, and all other traffic will be denied.

# EMAIL HARVESTING

Email Harvesting is the practice of gathering up valid email addresses for a target domain. Often times these can be used for reconnaissance, username enumeration, or to identify phishing and social engineering targets. This can be done manually by scraping a company's website, trawling through public records, or analyzing file metadata. However, there are tools that can do the initial time-consuming work for you, referred to as harvesting bots or harvesters.

## SOCIAL ENGINEERING

Social Engineering is when an attacker will psychologically manipulate someone into divulging information or performing a desired action. For example, someone without access to a server room might attempt to get in by saying that they forgot their badge at home.

**PHISHING:** When a social engineer conducts operations through email, this is referred to as "phishing." More broadly, phishing can refer to social engineering operations that involve any kind of electronic text or written exchange such as through cellular text and SMS messaging (referred to as "smishing"), through online social media, or through direct messaging and other real time chat programs and protocols.

The goal of a phishing operation is to elicit information or actions from the target. A social engineer might seek to elicit a direct action from the target, such as:

- Having the target type in their username and password.
- Having the target download and run malware on their computer.
- Having the target conduct specific actions, like wiring money to a fraudulent account.

More subtle forms of elicitation involve attempting to gain sensitive information from a target in order to further future attacks, such as personally identifiable information (PII), corporate intellectual property (IP), or logical and computing environmental information, such as security software and protections in use.

A phish has two core elements: the pretext and the elicitation. A target, whether consciously or subconsciously, will ask questions such as, "Why should I believe this message is coming from a trustworthy source?" and, "Why should I conduct the action requested by this message?" For this reason, the social engineer must craft an approach and message that establishes rapport and trust and follow that with a convincing call to action. For example, in order to establish rapport, a social engineer might pretend to be a person in authority, impersonate a known trusted entity, play on the target's vanity, or play on the target's desire for material gain. In order to convince the target to conduct an action, the social engineer might take advantage of a target's established habits or instill a sense of urgency.

In addition to psychological concepts and tools, a social engineer might also utilize technical tools and hacks to bolster their phish. In order to help establish pretext for a phish, a social engineer might send an email from a spoofed or fraudulent domain name, or send a message from a sockpuppet social media account designed to look like a known and trusted entity. The social engineer could also hack the target's email server or a secondary email account, and then send a legitimate email from that compromised account. The social engineer might even utilize a cloned login page, pointing the target towards a malicious site in order to capture credentials. This combination of technical hacking and psychological deceit increases the likelihood of a successful phishing operation.

**IMPERSONATION & INTERROGATION:** A social engineer interrogates a target in order to derive information. The desired information could be specific, such as the name of the antivirus software that is used on a computer, or it could be more general, like a discussion that covers which third party companies the target company is using for support. Specific information is used to advance predetermined and planned attacks, whereas general information is used to discover and suggest new attack vectors that have not been previously considered. An interrogation could either be direct and to the point, or it could be framed in a more casual and conversational tone.

Further, the attitude of an interrogation can be adversarial and hostile or more friendly and congenial. How a social engineer frames an interrogation depends on the social engineer's skill set and natural demeanor as well as the target's response to various techniques. When setting up a pretext (a believable fraudulent scenario) for an interrogation, a social engineer might chose to impersonate someone else. This assumed persona could be a real person that the target knows or knows of, or a fake person that holds a position that the target might respond favorably to. For instance, a social engineer might pretend to be the target's boss and send a fake email from the boss's email address. The target, believing the social engineer to be their boss, might conduct actions that they would not do if someone else asked them to do it. Likewise, a social engineer might pretend to be a nonexistent corporate auditor and convince the target to divulge critical information on company policies and procedures.

**CLOSE ACCESS:** Social engineering physically and in-person brings several considerations and tools to the table. Phishing is limited to text, and vishing (voice phishing) is limited to audio exchanges. Physical social engineering, however, allows a social engineer to use body language, microexpressions, and physical movements in addition to voice inflection during the operation.

Microexpressions and body language occur when a person expresses emotion, either voluntarily or involuntarily, with their body, face, or stance. A smile topped with crinkled eyes might convey happiness, though a smile with a tilted head and direct stare might convey annoyance. A social engineer uses microexpressions to elicit an emotional reaction from their target. They might laugh in order to build rapport or square off and face their target directly to convey a sense of authority. Conversely, a social engineer will read the microexpressions of their target to determine their emotional state or determine whether or not their target believes the social engineering pretext.

A social engineer uses bodily movement and close access to their target to physically guide their target's movement or their target's attention. A social engineer that moves into a target's personal space might cause the target to move away backwards, or they might walk behind a target who is opening a locked door and tailgate to step through the door with the target. A social engineer might use hand and face movements to distract a target or control the target's attention, much like a magician or a pickpocket. The social engineer can then conduct actions, like scanning an access badge or plugging in a USB filled with malware, without being noticed.

Another tool that a social engineer can take advantage of in physical situations is disguises. A disguise can be as simple as a change of clothes or as complex as makeup, prosthetics, and a wig. A disguise can be used to bolster a pretext. If a social engineer is posing as a construction worker, they might wear a hard hat and a high-vis vest. If a social engineer is posing as an auditor, they might wear a suit and carry a clipboard. A disguise can also be used to break up context during an operation. A social engineer might wear a long dark wig and glasses while physically conducting reconnaissance one day, only to come back the next day with a short blonde wig and no glasses to conduct actions on a target. This way, guards and employees will not associate the suspicious person from the day before with the person currently attempting to talk their way past security.

MOTIVATION: When attempting to elicit information or actions out of a target, a social engineer considers the target's motivations. A target's motivation to conduct an action could stem from a variety of reasons, such as a desire to gain personal wealth or power, a fear or intimidation, or a desire to help others. People have multiple motivators and a social engineer needs to consider unintended consequences of various approaches. Threatening a target may cause the target to move quickly and precisely, but may cause the target to remember and report the action to authorities after the operation. A target might react positively to a pretext that promises recognition, but it may take a while for the social engineer to build rapport and elicit action.

A person might be motivated by a desire for wealth, power, or attention. A social engineer that plays on this motivator might promise a target money if the target goes along with the scheme. For example, a social engineer might pledge to send a large amount of money if the target sends a small amount of money first, like an advanced-fee scam. For a longer term approach, a social engineer might pose as a representative agent promising to publish a book or further a target's project or cause. In this situation, the social engineer would build rapport with the target over time, only to elicit action or information from the target once the social engineer is trusted.

Intimidation or fear based motivators are used when the target has something to lose. A social engineer might threaten to release embarrassing information or photographs (either real or imagined) if the target does not comply with demands. These operations can be conducted remotely, such as via an extortion email, or in person, such as intimidating a target who has a smaller stature than the social engineer. Extortion, blackmail, and threats may cause some individuals to act quickly and precisely to the social engineer's demands, but this may cause the operation to be imprinted in the mind of the target. The target may then report the action to authorities afterwards causing the social engineer to be caught and stopped.

An opposite approach to using fear based motivators is to play on a target's desire to help other people. When the social engineer presents a pretext where they appear in need, the target might reach out and attempt to help. In a "grandparent scam," a social engineer poses as a grandchild who is in trouble. The target, wanting to help, wires money to a fraudulent account or performs some other action in order to protect the grandchild. During a physical close access operation, a social engineer might pose as a pregnant woman with their hands full in order to elicit a target to hold open a secured door for them. The more common, and day to day the interaction, such as a simple held door or a quick hug to clone a badge, the less likely the interaction will imprint on a target and the more likely the operation will evade detection.

## SOCIAL MEDIA PROFILING

Social Media Profiling is the process of collecting information about a target from their social media accounts using sites such as LinkedIn, Facebook, Instagram, or Twitter. This information could then be used for identity theft or for social engineering purposes.

Social Media Profiling, if used personally, can be taken too far and turn into cyber stalking. Be sure not to take your research so far as to begin cyber stalking someone, because that is illegal and could result in legal actions against you.

## DNS HARVESTING

DNS stands for Domain Name System. A DNS server translates domain names into IP addresses. DNS Harvesting is a way of enumerating domains and subdomains associated with a target. These tools can help an attacker identify hosts and services that are associated with a target and might have otherwise been missed.

The *harvester* is a great tool designed for DNS & Email harvesting:

```
➜ ~ theharvester -d kali.org -l 500 -b google
*******************************************************************
*                                                                 *
*   | |_| |__   ___  /\  /\__ _ _ ____   _____  ___| |_ ___ _ __  *
*   | __| '_ \ / _ \/ /_/ / _` | '__\ \ / / _ \/ __| __/ _ \ '__| *
*   | |_| | | |  __/ __  / (_| | |   \ V /  __/\__ \ ||  __/ |    *
*    \__|_| |_|\___\/ /_/ \__,_|_|    \_/ \___||___/\__\___|_|    *
*                                                                 *
* TheHarvester Ver. 2.7                                           *
* Coded by Christian Martorella                                   *
* Edge-Security Research                                          *
* cmartorella@edge-security.com                                   *
*******************************************************************

[-] Searching in Google:
        Searching 0 results...
        Searching 100 results...
        Searching 200 results...
        Searching 300 results...
        Searching 400 results...
        Searching 500 results...

[+] Emails found:
------------------
buxy@kali.org
devel@kali.org
st...@kali.org

[+] Hosts found in search engines:
------------------------------------
[-] Resolving hostnames IPs...
192.124.249.10:Www.kali.org
192.99.45.140:archive.kali.org
192.124.249.169:bugs.kali.org
192.99.200.113:cdimage.kali.org
192.124.249.10:docs.kali.org
192.124.249.12:forums.kali.org
67.23.72.103:git.kali.org
192.99.45.140:hera.kali.org
192.99.200.113:http.kali.org
54.39.49.227:old.kali.org
192.99.200.113:security.kali.org
192.124.249.6:tools.kali.org
192.124.249.10:www.kali.org
```

## TECHNOLOGICAL VARIABLES

### WIRELESS VS. WIRED

Most of the modern networks we're familiar with in our daily lives are wireless, but wired networks are still heavily used in enterprise environments. Wired networks use a physical medium such as cables to connect devices together, while wireless networks have no such requirement, allowing devices to freely move around an environment while staying connected to the network. Each of these come with their own set of advantages and constraints, but it's important to understand how they are used on a given network.

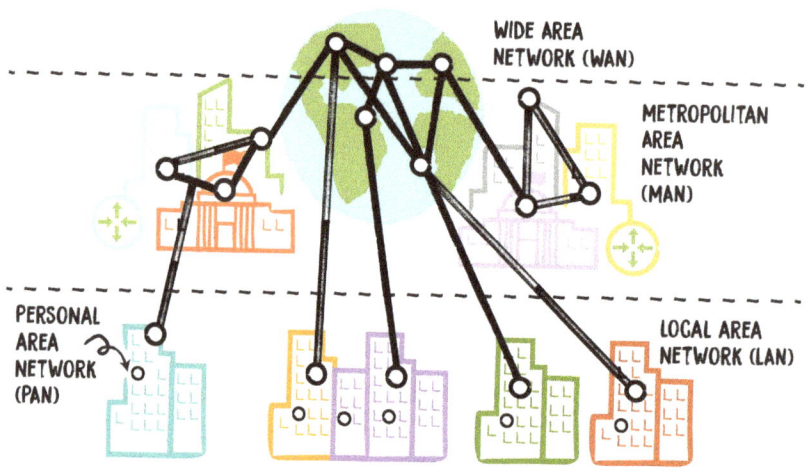

### VIRTUAL VS. PHYSICAL

A physical machine is a traditional computer acting as one machine running a single operating system on the network with full access to its own hardware resources. Virtualization allows a single physical machine to divide its resources amongst multiple virtual machines, each with their own set of resources, operating systems, and users. As you can imagine, this allows administrators to increase hardware utilization while reducing the cost and physical footprint required to run an enterprise network.

Virtualization always needs to be considered when trying to discover the topology of a network. It's important to remember one physical machine may actually be hosting multiple nodes on the network within it.

## ON-PREMISE VS. CLOUD

As SaaS (Software as a Service) continues to rise in popularity, it's important that IT and Security professionals remain aware of where their data physically resides. On-Premise means that the servers and data reside in a location you can control, like your company's server room. Cloud services often refer to services owned and managed by a third-party (e.g. Google or AWS) in a physical location you do not have access to.

## INTERNAL VS. EXTERNAL THREATS

External Threats are things like cyber-criminals who have no affiliation with a company trying to gain internal access to a network.

Insider Threats are those that come from within a company. One example of this would be if a disgruntled employee leaked information about a company to hurt its performance. Alternatively, poorly trained employees can be insider threats by accidentally damaging the security posture of the environment. An employee who accidentally deletes important information from a shared drive is a non-malicious insider threat. Consultants, part-time employees, volunteers, support service team members (HVAC techs, plumbers, drivers, security, parking attendants, etc.) who have access to facilities or the company's network can also pose potential insider threats.

## TOOLS

**NMAP:** An open source network discovery tool that makes it possible to scan an IP address, or a range of IP addresses, and see what responds to ICMP messages and what ports are open on those hosts. NMAP can also be used to detect which OS a machine is running and the version. NMAP will be discussed in greater depth later.

**HOST SCANNING:** This refers to a piece of software examining an individual host, looking for any software vulnerabilities or malware. One example of software with host scanning capabilities is Windows Defender, which monitors several areas of the computer looking for any changes due to malware or spyware.

```
bash-3.2# nmap -sS -sV -sC -Pn --script=vuln 10.100.2.10
Starting Nmap 7.80 ( https://nmap.org ) at 2019-08-14 20:37 CDT
Nmap scan report for                                    ı (
Host is up (0.044s latency).
Not shown: 998 filtered ports
PORT    STATE SERVICE  VERSION
80/tcp  open  http     Microsoft IIS httpd 7.5
|_clamav-exec: ERROR: Script execution failed (use -d to debug)
| http-aspnet-debug:
|_   status: DEBUG is enabled
| http-cross-domain-policy:
|   VULNERABLE:
|   Cross-domain and Client Access policies.
|     State: VULNERABLE
|       A cross-domain policy file specifies the permissions that a web client such as Java, Adobe Flash, Adobe Reader,
|       etc. use to access data across different domains. A client acces policy file is similar to cross-domain policy
|       but is used for M$ Silverlight applications. Overly permissive configurations enables Cross-site Request
|       Forgery attacks, and may allow third parties to access sensitive data meant for the user.
|
|     Check results:
|       /crossdomain.xml:
```

There are many different tools for host scanning including: Nessus, Zed Attack Proxy, and Retina. Nikto is another great web application vulnerability discovery tool that is often used in identifying vulnerabilities during pentests. An example of a Nikto scan can be seen below.

```
$ nikto -h http://10.100.2.10
- Nikto v2.1.6
---------------------------------------------------------------------------
+ Target IP:          10.100.2.10
+ Target Hostname:    10.100.2.10
+ Target Port:        80
+ Start Time:         2019-08-14 21:29:21 (GMT-5)
---------------------------------------------------------------------------
+ Server: Microsoft-IIS/7.5
+ Retrieved x-aspnet-version header: 4.0.30319
+ Retrieved x-powered-by header: ASP.NET
+ The anti-clickjacking X-Frame-Options header is not present.
+ The X-XSS-Protection header is not defined. This header can hint to the user agent to protect against some forms of XSS
+ The X-Content-Type-Options header is not set. This could allow the user agent to render the content of the site in a different fashion to the MIME type
+ Cookie AWSELB created without the httponly flag
+ Root page / redirects to: /pages/default.aspx?ReturnUrl=%2f
+ /clientaccesspolicy.xml contains a full wildcard entry. See http://msdn.microsoft.com/en-us/library/cc197955(v=vs.95).aspx
+ lines
+ OSVDB-630: IIS may reveal its internal or real IP in the Location header via a request to the /images directory. The value is "http://172.16.16.165/images/".
+ Allowed HTTP Methods: OPTIONS, TRACE, GET, HEAD, POST
+ Public HTTP Methods: OPTIONS, TRACE, GET, HEAD, POST
+ OSVDB-68127: Server is vulnerable to http://www.microsoft.com/technet/security/bulletin/MS10-070.asp allowing a cryptographic padding oracle.
+ OSVDB-3092: /pages/: This might be interesting...
+ OSVDB-3092: /Pages/: This might be interesting...
+ /Pages/default.aspx: FrontPage/Sharepointfile available.
+ 8328 requests: 0 error(s) and 15 item(s) reported on remote host
+ End Time:           2019-08-14 21:36:01 (GMT-5) (400 seconds)
```

**NETWORK MAPPING:** Network mapping is the act of discovering and representing the physical connections in a network. Once the physical devices in a network have been mapped discovering running software will be important for implementing protections.

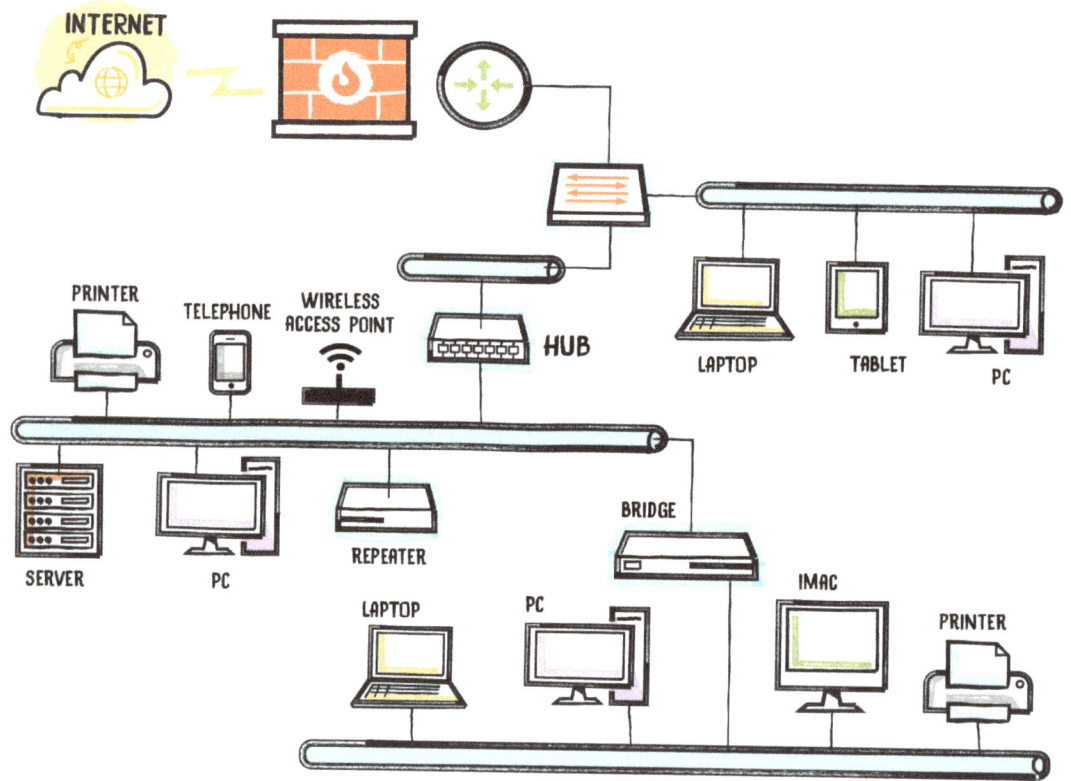

NETSTAT: Netstat is a tool that can display a host's network connections, open sockets, and other useful network statistics. It analyzes network traffic on a specific host interface and can display things such as active TCP and UDP connections that host has. This can be used to see if a host is connected to or communicating with something it shouldn't be. Netstat is on windows, Linux, and mac operating systems. and it has many additional functions, such as showing routes. Someone troubleshooting network connections might running *netstat -rn* :

```
goliath@active-io:~$ netstat -rn
Kernel IP routing table
Destination     Gateway         Genmask         Flags   MSS Window  irtt Iface
0.0.0.0         10.100.2.10     0.0.0.0         UG        0 0          0 ens160
10.100.2.0      0.0.0.0         255.255.255.0   U         0 0          0 ens160
goliath@active-io:~$
```

## PACKET ANALYZER

A packet analyzer is software that can give a user information about individual packets. These can also be referred to as packet sniffers. TCP packets do not always arrive in order, and so a packet analyzer will reorder these packets so they are easier for people to read. Also, packet analyzers will allow users to organize information in a way that is helpful to them, such as reading packets from a specific TCP connection, rather than sifting through thousands for some other connection.

## IDS / IPS

Intrusion Detection Systems (IDSs) detect and alert on suspect network traffic, which is a passive process. They typically use Deep Packet Inspection (DPI) to analyze the full packet or stream of packets against a set of known signatures or behavior heuristics. Snort and Suricata are open-source IDS solutions that use a signature-based approach, while Zeek (formerly known as Bro Network Security Monitor) uses heuristics to identify suspect traffic. Software applications like NMAP can produce traffic that will trigger an appropriately configured IDS.

Intrusion Prevention Systems (IPSs) also alert on network traffic, but can additionally take action on suspect network traffic. This is an active process which requires the IPS device to be installed inline on the network.

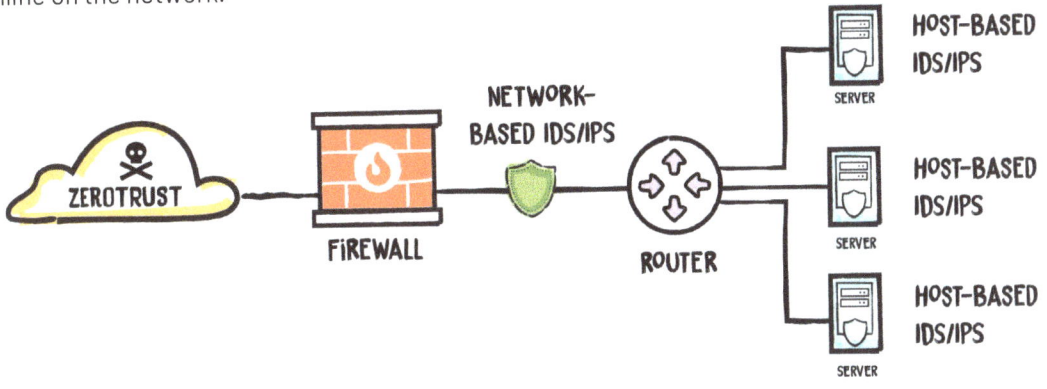

## HIDS / NIDS

An Intrusion Detection System (IDS) can be either host-based or network-based.

Network Intrusion Detection Systems (NIDS) ingest network traffic, while analyzing and reporting suspicious activity back to an administrator. This is done by placing sensors on the network which collect the data packets and forward them back to the NIDS appliance for analysis.

Host-based Intrusion Detection Systems (HIDS) reside on a specific host and can monitor that host's network traffic, system processes, file creation events and user activity. These systems use the software on individual hosts as the sensors which provide the IDS functionality.

## FIREWALL RULE-BASED & LOGS

Rule-based firewalls are firewalls that use rules to determine whether or not traffic can pass through them. These rules operate on an access control list and specifically list out how traffic from certain addresses should be handled. Rule-based firewalls will produce logs that document what traffic passed through, was blocked, and which rule was used to specify this.

## SYSLOG

Syslog, as mentioned earlier, is a logging standard which enables devices to produce event messages whenever actions take place on the device. Examining these messages can allow administrators to view important historical system events. These can be either analyzed on the devices themselves, or they can be sent to a centralized syslog server. The syslog server stores all log files so that an analyst only has to look at one server, rather than every network device on a network.

## VULNERABILITY SCANNER

This software scans individual hosts or networks for vulnerabilities. There are a couple ways to go about scanning for vulnerabilities. The first is to use NMAP to scan for open ports on operating systems. For example, if port 445 is open on Microsoft Directory Services, you could research OS specific vulnerabilities for that service to use against the host machine.

Another way to do this is to use a piece of software that is dedicated to vulnerability scanning, such as Nessus. Nessus can scan a network for things like missing patches, blank/absent or default/weak passwords used on accounts, and misconfigurations that could open the system to an attacker.

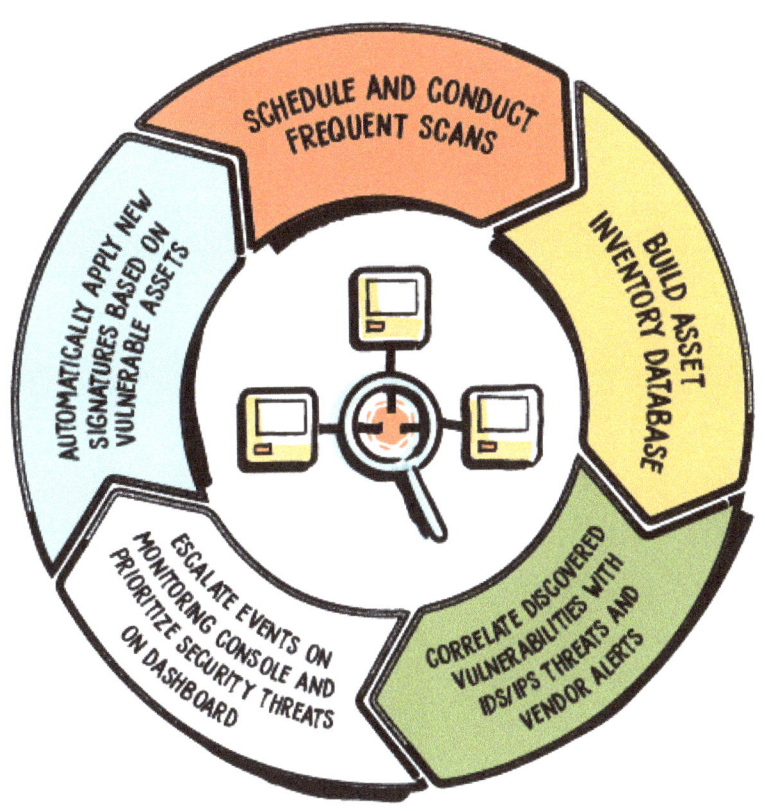

# RECONNAISSANCE RESULTS

## POINT-IN-TIME & DATA CORRELATION / ANALYTICS

Point-in-time analysis is the practice of storing snapshots of information into a database for later analysis. Analysts can use this information to later construct a picture of what was going on in a network at any given time.

## PACKET, PROTOCOL, & TRAFFIC ANALYSIS

Packet analysis involves using a packet sniffer, such as Wireshark, to examine captured packets. Packet analysis is a type of point-in-time analysis because it can be used to reconstruct and analyze what happened at a specific time. This can be done by filtering the packet analyzer to display packets that came through in a specific timeframe.

A protocol analyzer is a software tool that can intercept and then display and organize packets based on the protocols used. Like packet analysis, Wireshark can also do protocol analysis.

Both methods can be used to analyze traffic for a picture of what happened at a particular time.

## NETFLOW ANALYSIS

NetFlow analysis allows an administrator to see all traffic passing through their network. NetFlow records are often generated by a firewall or switch on the network and provide summary records about network traffic that include details such as source, destination, protocol, the number of packets, and the amount of bytes transferred. These records can then be sent to other tools for reporting and analysis. Administrators may also have them open to sample a small subset of network traffic in order to fine-tune analysis and save resources on production network devices.

## WIRELESS ANALYSIS

Once the packet is captured, wireless analysis happens in much the same way as LAN packet analysis happens. However, because wireless networks are often used to allow guests to hop onto a network, there are different tools for analyzing wireless traffic data. One of these tools is Solarwinds' wireless network monitor tool, which can help to detect rogue devices on a network, analyze peak traffic times, and wireless availability over time. Special hardware tools exist which are suited for capturing wireless packets, though the most common solution can be achieved by putting a standard wireless card into promiscuous mode, enabling captures on normal PCs.

## DATA CORRELATION & ANALYTICS

Once the data is collected, there are several techniques for better understanding the data.

**ANOMALY ANALYSIS:** A system performing anomaly analysis will first establish what normal traffic looks like over time, and then flag unusual traffic as an anomaly. This can help detect malicious traffic on a network.

**TREND ANALYSIS:** A system that analyzes trends looks at current and past trends in an effort to predict the future. Trend analysis can be used to identify an increase in daily traffic on a network, and thus be used to guide companies to invest in new infrastructure.

**AVAILABILITY ANALYSIS:** Simply analyzing the availability of different services. An unexplained downtime in availability can point to an issue that needs to be further explored.

**SIGNATURE ANALYSIS:** Running software through a hashing algorithm creates a signature unique to that software. This signature is known as a "fingerprint". Anytime a new piece of malware is discovered, its signature is added to a database. Signature analysis compares all fingerprints on a network to those on a malware database. If a matching signature is discovered, malware is on the network.

**HEURISTIC, OR BEHAVIORAL ANALYSIS:** Heuristic analysis is when a system is analyzed for its behavior, or what it does. This can be important in identifying a piece of malware that is not detected by signature analysis on a network, though it does require a baselining period, for identifying typical network usage.

## DATA OUTPUT, TOOLS

A lot of the reconnaissance work that we have talked about so far relies on using tools to understand what is going on in a network. However, this information is meaningless unless the output is understandable. This section will go through some of the common data output.

## SYSLOG & DIFFERENT TYPES OF LOGS

Syslog is a logging standard that allows many different devices to generate log messages that can be centrally stored and analyzed, typically on a Syslog Server. As we'll cover later, each log contains a field identifying where it came from, what time it occurred, it's importance or severity, and any other details the log originator chooses to include.

Event logs capture events that an administrator might want to audit later. These include things like a user's resource and right usage, login events, when files are edited, when applications are set up, and when traffic is allowed / not allowed to go through a network device.

A firewall is one such device that generates logs that may be sent to a syslog server. Firewalls can be set up to document when traffic is allowed or denied to pass through them. Log entries can have different severity levels, allowing users to easily see which entries are most important.

As you can imagine, getting logs for all of these levels on a large network would result in a lot of information. Because of this, some networks are set to log only certain levels, such as level 0, for emergencies. Others are set up to log everything.

Cisco log messages use the following format. "Warning" is Cisco's default reporting level:

| LEVEL | DESCRIPTION |
| --- | --- |
| 0 - emergency | System unusable |
| 1 - alert | Immediate action needed |
| 2 - critical | Critical condition |
| 3 - error | Error condition |
| 4 - warning | Warning condition |
| 5 - notification | Normal but significant condition |
| 6 - informational | Informational message only |
| 7 - debugging | Appears during debugging only |

```
seq no:timestamp: %facility-severity-MNEMONIC:description
```

The sequence number simply identifies that log entry. Then, the timestamp identifies when the event occurred. Then, the severity mnemonic gives a severity level, as listed above, along with a description of that severity. The description part defines what was logged.

Here is an example of a system log message:

```
111: April 29 12:11:44.190 UTC: %SEC-6-IPACCESSLOGP: list 199 permitted tcp
192.168.3.11(1477) -> 10.0.0.33(445), 1 packet
112: April 29 12:13:54.422 UTC: %SEC-6-IPACCESSLOGP: list 199 denied tcp
192.168.3.13(1477) -> 10.0.0.33(1060), 1 packet
```

At first glance a message like this might be hard to digest. Let's break this one down.

First, notice the numbers 111 and 112. These are the two sequence numbers for this log file. So, there are two log files being looked at here.

The second piece of information on these two log files is the timestamp. Both of these were recorded on April 29. One was at 12:11, and the other at 12:13.

These are both IP access logs, which means they will relay an IP communication that was either permitted or denied.

The last part of each of these messages is the description. Let's first look at the description for 111. It says, "list 199 permitted tcp 192.168.3.11(1477) -> 10.0.0.33(445), 1 packet." This means that tcp traffic from 192.168.3.11 over port 1477 was permitted to go to the IP address 10.0.0.33 to port 445.

For 112, the description says, "list 199 denied tcp 109.4.3.13(1477) -> 10.0.0.33(1060), 1 packet." This means that TCP traffic from 109.4.3.12 on port 1477 was not permitted to go to 10.0.0.33 on port 1060.

It's important to note that there are a lot of different kinds of logs, from router logs to firewall logs. There are also a lot of different manufacturers, like Cisco, Palo Alto, and Check Point. Be aware that these log files may look a little different, but they will still have the same information. All log files should have a date/time stamp and a section that shows details. All of the details should look similar to the details listed above, including actions taken and the IP / MAC addresses on which those actions were taken.

## PACKET ANALYZERS & OUTPUT FROM PACKET CAPTURES

Wireshark allows users to look at specific packets in a network and organize the traffic in many different ways. For instance, a user can look at packets temporarily, from specific IP addresses, packets involved in a single TCP session, and in countless other ways. Here is a screenshot of a Wireshark capture:

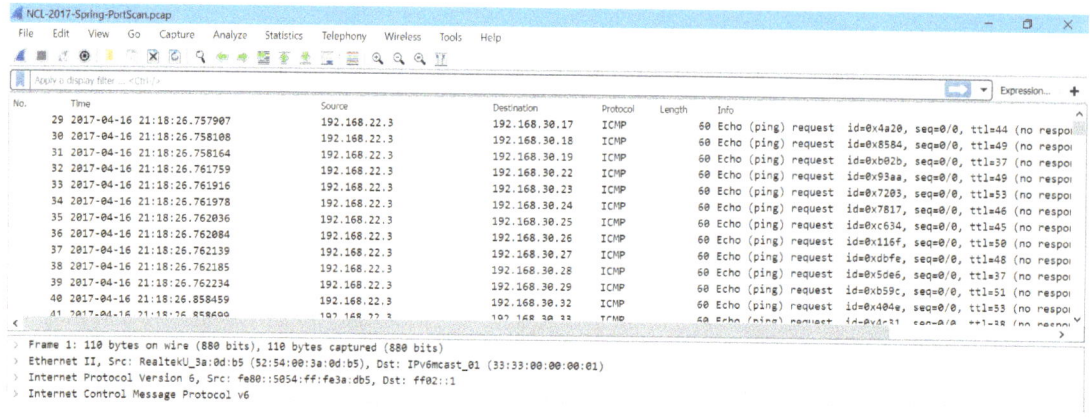

There's a lot of information in this capture. For the moment, let's focus on the top white box.

The time column displays the time of the event, while the source and destination columns display the source and destination IP addresses. The protocol for all of these packets is ICMP.

Viewing these packets, it's easy to see that source 192.168.22.3 is pinging a sequence of IP addresses. This could be to see which machines respond to determine the network's topology.

# NMAP

This open source tool allows users to get a map of a network, find ports running on a computer, and see services running on some computers. NMAP can be used for security auditing and also for discovery. Here is an example of a basic NMAP scan, in which the IP address 1.2.3.4 is examined:

```
root@kali:~# nmap 1.2.3.4

Starting Nmap 7.01 ( https://nmap.org ) at 2018-04-28 11:18 EDT
Nmap scan report for 1.2.3.4
Host is up (0.5s latency).
Not shown: 998 closed ports
PORT            STATE           SERVICE
22/TCP          open            ssh
80/TCP          open            http
```

The scan of this IP address reveals that it has two ports open, 22 for SSH and 80 for HTTP. This is the most basic way to use the NMAP command.

By using NMAP, it is also possible to ping all hosts in a network and see which respond. Here is an example of using NMAP to ping the 1.2.3.0/24 network to see which hosts reside on it.

```
root@kali:~# nmap 1.2.3.0/24

Starting Nmap 7.01 ( https://nmap.org ) at 2018-04-28 11:18 EDT
Nmap scan report for 1.2.3.4
Host is up (0.002s latency).
MAC Address: 00:0C:12:8A:44:8B (VMWARE)
```

There are also a number of different flags that can be used to alter an NMAP scan. These include:

```
-O flag: This flag will reveal what operating system is being used.
-sV: This flag does version detection.
-sS: This is a flag to do a SYN (stealth) scan so that the NMAP scanner is less likely to be detected.
```

NMAP is not always a complete solution for viewing the topology of a network. Firewalls can use ACLs to block certain traffic, and some ACLs can block NMAP scans, thus preventing NMAP from learning about the network. Virtual networks can also be a challenge for NMAP. It may be possible to see servers with virtual machines on them, but not to see the actual virtual hosts themselves.

## IDS & IDS REPORT

Intrusion detection systems give output that lets the user know that there has been network activity and indicates that an intruder might be present.

A firewall performs a similar function, but uses different means. A firewall looks at traffic that is passing through it and will deny or allow it based on certain rules. IDS's analyze traffic within the network by using signatures or heuristics to discover unusual communication. Consider this output from an IDS report from Snort, a NIDS software:

| ALERT ID | DATE/TIME | SOURCE | DESTINATION | EVENT MESSAGE |
| --- | --- | --- | --- | --- |
| 2.4 | 2018-5-3 07:55 | 69.68.13.20 (6765) | 192.168.1.20 (135) | ET SCAN Behavioral Unusual Port 135 traffic, Potential Scan or Infection |

This alert lets an administrator know that unusual traffic has been detected inside of the network.

**SIEM:** This stands for security information event manager. A SIEM takes in data from a variety of places, such as syslog servers and netflow analyzers, and then allow users to do data analysis, correlate, build graphs, and alert on the data that they have received from all of these devices.

SIEMs are not simply log aggregation systems; they also generate reports to help administrators better understand what is happening on the network. SIEMs can also do event and data analysis to look for security issues in the network.

**RESOURCE MONITORING TOOL:** There are many resource monitoring tools. The most common of these is a simple host activity monitor, like the one that comes with all Mac and PC operating systems. Here is an example of the Mac output, which shows processes, how many threads the processes are using, and what percentage of CPU those processes are utilizing:

| Process Name | % CPU | CPU Time | Threads | Idle Wake Ups | PID | User |
|---|---|---|---|---|---|---|
| screencapture | 3.6 | 0.34 | 2 | 0 | 2217 | williamleito |
| Activity Monitor | 1.7 | 6.35 | 5 | 3 | 2208 | williamleito |
| https://apps.google.com, … | 0.3 | 6:32.23 | 7 | 2 | 1492 | williamleito |
| Safari Networking | 0.1 | 45.55 | 5 | 1 | 1465 | williamleito |
| SafariBookmarksSyncAgent | 0.0 | 4.18 | 4 | 2 | 435 | williamleito |
| SafariCloudHistoryPushAgent | 0.0 | 1.19 | 3 | 1 | 1473 | williamleito |
| CommCenter | 0.0 | 2.35 | 8 | 2 | 343 | williamleito |
| Google Chrome Helper | 0.0 | 0.29 | 15 | 1 | 2215 | williamleito |
| Google Chrome | 0.0 | 6:28.80 | 40 | 1 | 742 | williamleito |
| universalaccessd | 0.0 | 0.95 | 3 | 1 | 341 | williamleito |
| Google Chrome Helper | 0.0 | 2:35.57 | 10 | 0 | 928 | williamleito |
| nsurlstoraged | 0.0 | 6.70 | 3 | 0 | 361 | williamleito |
| Safari | 0.0 | 2:28.68 | 6 | 1 | 1457 | williamleito |
| http://manual-snort-org.s3-… | 0.0 | 18.71 | 6 | 0 | 1912 | williamleito |
| parsecd | 0.0 | 4.77 | 4 | 0 | 535 | williamleito |
| https://support.apple.com | 0.0 | 22.19 | 10 | 2 | 2142 | williamleito |
| loginwindow | 0.0 | 4.30 | 2 | 1 | 117 | williamleito |
| Photos Agent | 0.0 | 1.67 | 5 | 1 | 370 | williamleito |
| assistantd | 0.0 | 1.28 | 3 | 1 | 418 | williamleito |
| distnoted | 0.0 | 11.96 | 2 | 1 | 335 | williamleito |
| Dock | 0.0 | 3.26 | 3 | 1 | 746 | williamleito |
| Messages | 0.0 | 4.46 | 6 | 0 | 744 | williamleito |
| iTunes Networking | 0.0 | 1.22 | 4 | 1 | 1254 | williamleito |
| iTunes | 0.0 | 10.16 | 23 | 2 | 743 | williamleito |
| nbagent | 0.0 | 1.11 | 5 | 0 | 368 | williamleito |
| sharingd | 0.0 | 7.69 | 3 | 1 | 379 | williamleito |
| nsurlsessiond | 0.0 | 4.66 | 5 | 1 | 346 | williamleito |
| Notification Center | 0.0 | 3.19 | 3 | 1 | 378 | williamleito |
| OSDUIHelper | 0.0 | 1.30 | 3 | 0 | 953 | williamleito |
| AirPlayUIAgent | 0.0 | 0.42 | 3 | 0 | 785 | williamleito |
| Finder | 0.0 | 2.89 | 3 | 0 | 748 | williamleito |
| com.apple.geod | 0.0 | 0.93 | 4 | 1 | 393 | williamleito |
| ckkeyrolld | 0.0 | 0.42 | 3 | 0 | 774 | williamleito |
| commerce | 0.0 | 1.31 | 4 | 0 | 426 | williamleito |
| Wi-Fi | 0.0 | 0.56 | 5 | 0 | 365 | williamleito |
| com.apple.Safari.SafeBrowsi… | 0.0 | 1.65 | 2 | 1 | 1490 | williamleito |
| Safari Storage | 0.0 | 0.55 | 5 | 0 | 1491 | williamleito |
| AssetCacheLocatorService | 0.0 | 0.46 | 4 | 0 | 498 | williamleito |
| talagent | 0.0 | 0.60 | 2 | 0 | 421 | williamleito |

| | | CPU LOAD | | |
|---|---|---|---|---|
| System: | 2.35% | | Threads: | 1286 |
| User: | 2.45% | | Processes: | 360 |
| Idle: | 95.20% | | | |

**NETFLOW ANALYZER:** NetFlow analyzers are tools that can display network bandwidth usage. "NetFlow" is a Cisco protocol that analyzes and monitors network traffic.

There are many different ways that netflow analyzers can display data to a user. One way is to view IP traffic by the different IP addresses on the network. Another way a netflow analyzer can share data to a user is to show which protocols are using the most data:

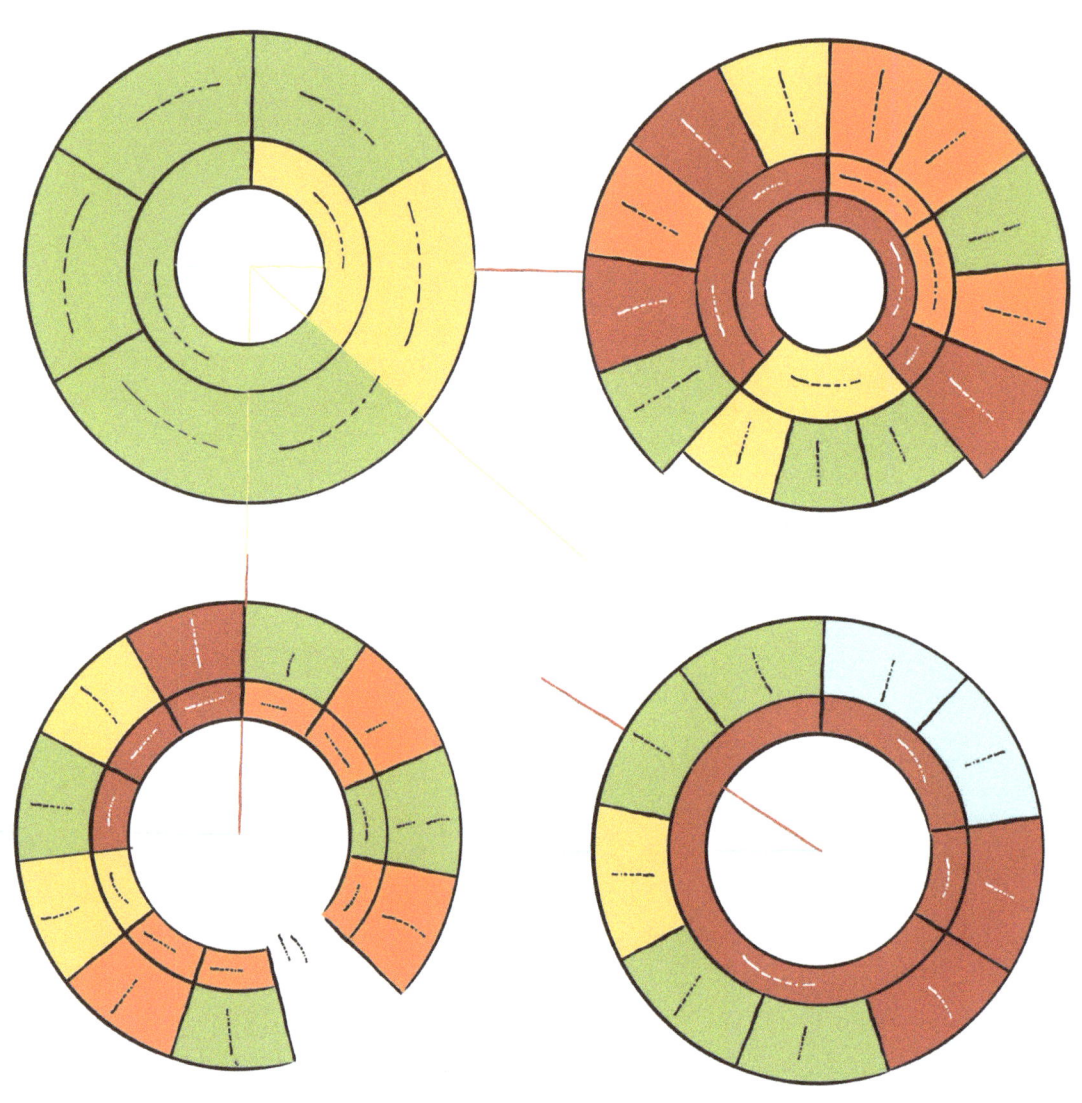

# NETWORK BASED THREAT MITIGATION

## NETWORK SEGMENTATION

At its simplest, network segmentation splits up a network with firewalls. For example:

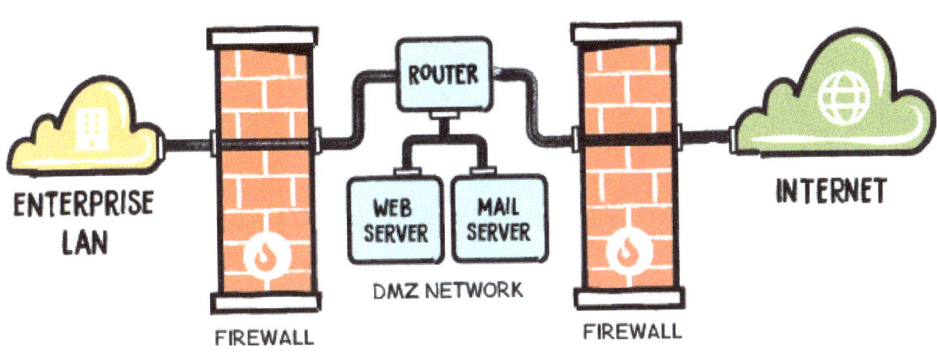

However, networks can be segmented even further. For example, consider an intranet where there are user workstations and a database with sensitive information:

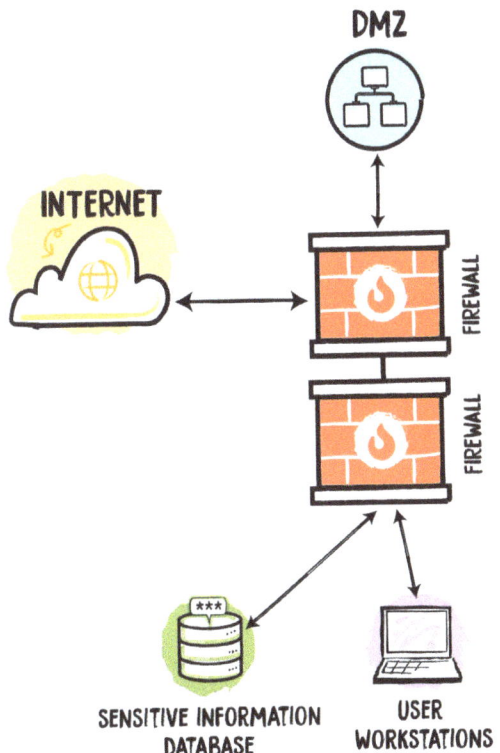

Network segmentation occurs any time that a network is divided up by a firewall. Segmenting the network further by adding a firewall between the user workstations and the database makes the network more secure. This prevents malevolent actors who gain access to a user workstation from accessing the entire network.

## JUMP SERVER

A jump server, also called a "jump box", is a server that isolates two systems or networks so they don't have to communicate directly. This is important when users need to access highly sensitive information in a database, and the administrator would like to monitor the requests that are being made to the database.

If the jump server sits between users and a database, then the user's host is never in direct communication with that database. In this scenario, users make requests to the jump server, which sends requests to the database, and the jump server returns the information to the user.

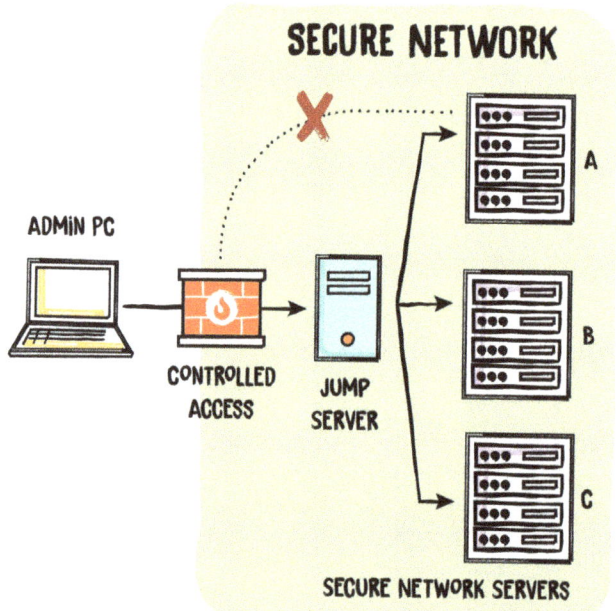

Additionally a jump server could require engineers / operators to 'jump' to a certain machine before they are allowed to manage another portion of the network. This is a common network segmentation technique used by organizations with critical infrastructures.

This is a typical strategy for securing management access to devices. Instead of allowing a large portion of the network to access the management plane, all access can easily be controlled and monitored through a jump server. This can make it easier to secure access to the management environment while also having a central location for logs pertaining to management access.

# NETWORK ACCESS CONTROL

Network Access Control (NAC) is a solution that helps organizations or users decide who is or isn't allowed to connect to a network. NAC systems essentially ensure that a computer is approved to be on a network before access is allowed. When securing a network, it is important to control who is on it. It would be a bad practice if someone could park their car beside an organization's building and instantly access their wireless network. Likewise, it would be bad if someone who entered an organization's building could simply plug their computer into an ethernet port and gain access to the network. For this reason, there are two main types of network access control:

**AGENT-BASED:** An agent based NAC system requires that the device attempting to connect to the network is running certain software for properly authentication. In the case of 802.1x (which is an agent-based NAC solution), this piece of software is called the supplicant.

**AGENTLESS:** This is the opposite of agent-based solutions. With agentless NAC, the connecting computer does not need special software; for example, a coffee shop might have a simple web page that allows visitors to sign in and connect to the wifi shop's network. One way to do that is the 802.1x protocol.

In an 802.1x system, there is a supplicant, an authenticator, and a RADIUS server, as shown:

The supplicant is a piece of software that is running on a computer trying to connect to a network. The supplicant communicates with the authenticator, which then communicates with the RADIUS server to try to validate the supplicant. The supplicant cannot communicate with the RADIUS server directly, and so has to use the authenticator as a proxy.

The supplicant will send its credentials to the authenticator, which then sends those to the RADIUS server. If the RADIUS server deems these acceptable, it will send a message to the authenticator, which will allow the supplicant to connect to the network.

Additionally, there are two more ways that NAC solutions can be divided further:

**IN-BAND:** This refers to a computer that is trying to connect gets inside of a network, but is in a separate area. An example of this would be a coffee shop's sign-in page.

**OUT-OF-BAND:** With NAC solutions such as 802.1x, computers that have not been authenticated are actually in a separate network before the RADIUS server validates them. This is an example of an out-of-band NAC solution.

With all of these variations, we still haven't talked about what a computer might need to do to get onto a NAC network. Here are some considerations to determine if a computer should be granted access to a computer:

**TIME OF DAY:** An organization may not allow new connections in the middle of the night.

**LOCATION:** Some organizations may not allow a computer to connect to a certain service if it is in an improper location. For example, an organization might say that people can only log on to a network from their work or home.

**ROLE:** A network may be configured to give some people access to some systems, while not others. For example, in a university, the network may be configured so as to not allow any non-faculty members to access a database of student grades.

**SYSTEM HEALTH:** An organization could make a rule with criteria for computer configurations that are logging on. For example, they may only allow computers with certain patches, operating systems, or software to log on.

# HARDENING, HONEYPOTS, ENDPOINT SECURITY, & GROUPS POLICIES

## MANDATORY ACCESS CONTROL

Mandatory access control (MAC) is a type of control in which a subject's ability to access or modify different objects is constrained.

MAC is often found in very secure environments. With MAC, each person on a system is given levels of security access. Data is also given security levels. If a user's security level isn't high enough, he or she cannot access that data.

## COMPENSATING CONTROLS

A compensating control does not remove a risk, it simply mitigates it. Sometimes, it is undesirable or impossible to completely remove all risks with endpoints. For example, if a printer had a known vulnerability in its software that uses port 5555, but it would be expensive to fix the vulnerability, an organization could use a firewall rule to block port 5555 to compensate for that vulnerability.

## BLOCKING UNUSED PORTS / SERVICES

When a service isn't being used on a computer, it's best to block the corresponding port. The reason is simple: Disabling an unused port will not decrease availability, but it will decrease the amount of attacks that could be used on the network. For example, if a machine on the network does not need to have SSH capabilities, it is a good idea to block port 22.

## PATCHING

Through the lifecycle of applications and operating systems, new vulnerabilities and flaws are discovered. To fix these problems and defend the system from hackers, it's important to patch the systems. A patch is a piece of software that can take care of vulnerabilities or functional issues.

Since networks often have many different systems on them, it's best to use a patch management system. A patch management system can scan the network for applications and OSs running on it, and it can automatically update the systems.

## HONEYPOT

Honeypots are systems designed to lure attackers into wasting time and attention on a target of no value while also alerting an administrator to their presence. For example, an organization may set up a file sharing server that looks like it has sensitive information (e.g. HR records, passwords, or financial data) hoping to entice attackers into accessing those files, thus triggering an alert. When implemented correctly, this provides a high-confidence way to detect attackers on your network and observe how they operate.

## ENDPOINT SECURITY

The devices that people use to connect to a network present another source of security threats to that network. These devices, such as tablets, phones and computers, are called endpoints. A misconfigured endpoint on a system can make a network vulnerable.

**HARDENING SYSTEM CONFIGURATIONS:** This means dictating system configurations to all of the endpoints in the network. These include blocking unnecessary port numbers or services from endpoints on the network and making sure that all of the endpoints on the network have up to date security configurations.

**PATCH MANAGEMENT:** This refers to ensuring that all of the endpoints are installing patches properly. Often, a company such as Microsoft will release a patch to fix a vulnerability it has. Ensuring that all endpoints on a network have up to date patches is a good way to increase security and is enhanced by vulnerability scanning.

**EDITING GROUP POLICIES:** Group policy objects (GPOs) allow managers to push system security configurations to many devices on a network. Utilizing this, a manager could make it such that all Windows computers must have certain firewall settings to be on the network.

**ENDPOINT SECURITY SOFTWARE:** This refers to the types of software that can run on endpoints to increase the security of the network. For example, this could include antivirus software and intrusion detection system software.

# CORPORATE SECURITY BEST PRACTICES

## PENETRATION TESTING

Penetration testing (also referred to as 'pen testing') is a process in which someone working for an organization simulates an attack on the network to test the effectiveness of the security measures in place. These penetration testers will then report the findings to the organization so that any vulnerabilities discovered can be managed. There are several different phases of a penetration test.

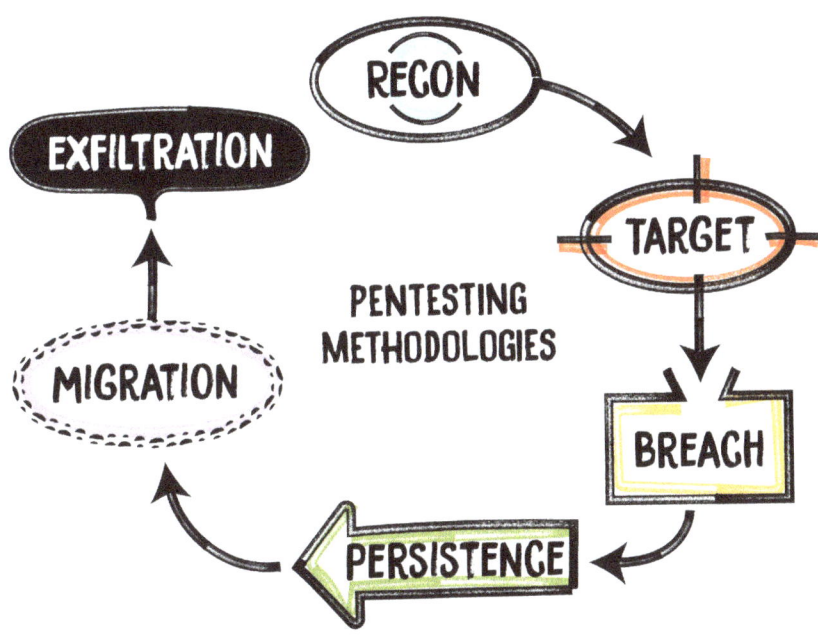

**PHASE 1: PLANNING** Since there are many ways for a penetration test to be carried out, ground rules must be in place before any penetration test can be started.

First, it needs to be determined what time the pen test will take place. This could be a specified block of hours or a larger frame of time. It should also be discussed if the staff should know that a penetration test is taking place. Depending on the goals, the staff may or may not be alerted.

The scope should also be agreed upon beforehand. This is to delineate what is okay for the pen testers to try to attack, and what systems they may not attack. Penetration testers who operate out of their agreed upon scope may be held legally responsible for violations. Additionally, pen testing a third-party with whom the target has a relationship is typically out of scope as well.

Lastly, but perhaps most importantly, the test's authorization should be planned. Before initiating a pen test, the testers should know who authorized them to test, and who they should report to if they are caught. Without a contract, pen testing is illegal. This is why it is important to obtain clear authorization. Understanding valid targets is a critical skill for a security analyst.

**PHASE 2: DISCOVERY** This is when the penetration testers do reconnaissance work on the network or organization to determine the best way to attack. This phase is broad and includes anything that the pen testers might do to prepare for the attack, like researching the company online, identifying company resources that might be part of their attack, conducting service and vulnerability scans on the network, and any other means of gathering information.

**PHASE 3: ATTACK** This is the phase where the penetration testers are actually trying to gain access and perhaps modify a system. There are four phases of the attack phase that should be followed in order:
1. **GAIN ACCESS:** This is when the penetration testers try to get initial access to a system using the information gathered in the discovery phase.
2. **ESCALATING PRIVILEGES:** This is when the penetration tester has access to a system, but wants to see if he/she can escalate their privileges to administrator-level access to gain complete control of the system.
3. **PIVOTING & NETWORK MIGRATION:** This is when the penetration testers look into other peripheral systems and do reconnaissance on them. This is similar to discovery, but it happens after the pen testers already have some access.

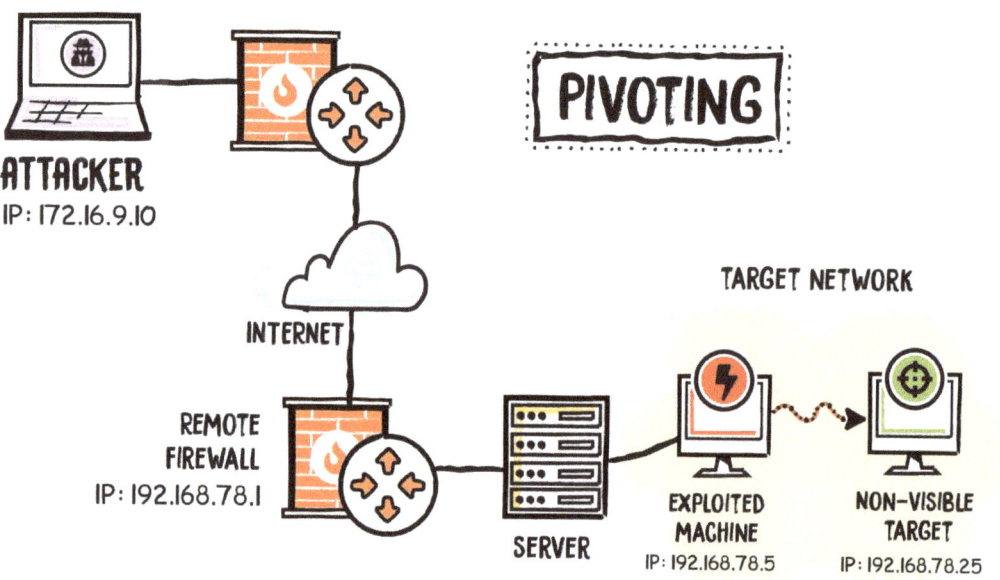

**PHASE 4: REPORT** After the attack phase, the penetration testers will typically write a report for their customers. These reports detail which attacks were successful, as well as what was unsuccessful, with suggestions for how to mitigate found vulnerabilities.

## TRAINING & EXERCISES

For training purposes, a company may have one group of individuals set up a network and another group attack it. This is a great way to train individuals how to respond to various scenarios within their organization and identify organizational weaknesses. It is important to understand a few terms that may be used going forward:

**RED TEAM:** In a simulated war game, the red team plays the role of the attacker. They try to gain access to the other team's network.

**BLUE TEAM:** This team is responsible for protecting the target environment. They might need to adjust firewall rules or install patches to keep the red team out.

**WHITE TEAM:** The white team referees in cybersecurity wargames. They set up the rules and environment and make sure that the games are going about fairly.

These names do not just apply to cybersecurity wargames, however. For instance, there are organizations that use "red teams" to describe their team of pen testers. Also, the term blue team can be used to describe individuals who work to protect a network.

## REVERSE ENGINEERING

Reverse engineering is the act of looking at a completed project to determine how it works. This could involve taking the product apart, analyzing components, or simply examining it. Almost anything can be reverse engineered, from an airplane to a car.

In cybersecurity, professionals often reverse engineer malware to better understand what it does, how it was built, and who might have built it. Malware authors want to obfuscate their code in such a way that makes it much harder to detect and analyze. This makes it necessary for cybersecurity professionals to reverse engineer the malware to understand what it does, but before the malware can be reverse engineered, it must be observed to see how it operates. Dynamic Analysis involves executing the malware in a sandbox environment while observing and logging what it does. Static Analysis, on the other hand, is analyzing the malware's code without actually executing it.

## SANDBOXING

Sandboxing is the practice of taking an application out of the network so that it can be tested. It can be dangerous to test a piece of malware on a computer inside of the network, so it's best to run it on a virtual machine or some other type of isolated environment. There, professionals can observe the application's behavior in order to understand what it does.

It's also good to note that sandboxing can also be an automated process. Some applications will automatically take any unusual code out of the network and run it in an environment to see what it does. It may then report the code to a human for further analysis.

## REVERSE ENGINEERING HARDWARE

It may be necessary for cybersecurity professionals to reverse engineer hardware to see if it has been tampered with. This is an extremely difficult thing to do because of how complicated the machinery is and the interactions it has with the firmware.

When reverse engineering hardware, it is important to look for source authenticity, which means that the hardware has not been tampered with and can be trusted.

Though it is difficult to do at times, when it is necessary to reverse engineer hardware it may be necessary to contact the original equipment manufacturers (OEMs) to get documentation about the hardware.

## THE CIA TRIAD

The CIA Triad consists of confidentiality, integrity, and availability. These represent the top level cybersecurity objectives.

**CONFIDENTIALITY:** The principal that unauthorized users should not have access to sensitive information. In striving for confidentiality, a cybersecurity professional may use both physical and electronic means of protecting sensitive information. Physical means would include things such as locked server rooms, ID badges to grant access to a building, cameras to monitor areas where sensitive information is held, and other security measures. Electronic means of securing sensitive information would include things such as passwords, firewalls, and intelligence.

**INTEGRITY:** The principle that information should not be modified unless the modification is authorized. For example, if someone is able to change the price of items in an online store to zero, then order and receive free items, the price alteration would be a breach of integrity.

**AVAILABILITY:** This is measured in up time. This is dependent on how available a service is to do what it is intended to do. For example, if an online store's website is down, this is an undesirable availability. Denial of service attacks are an example of an attack that can limit availability.

**NON-REPUDIATION:** While not a part of the traditional CIA triad, this is an important concept to understand in conjunction. This is the act of ensuring that an action taken by an actor is traceable back to the person. Unique user accounts are one way to promote non-repudiation in a system.

## TYPES OF THREATS

A threat is intent to damage or hostile action against systems. There are four types of threats:

1. **ADVERSARIAL THREATS:** From actors that intentionally try to harm an organization. These can be a wide range of actors, from script kitties that might cause harm to gain notoriety, to business competitors trying to make an uneven competitive playing field.
2. **ACCIDENTAL THREATS:** These occur when a user accidentally does something that undermines security. An example would be someone inside of the company accidentally turning off a web server, which then decreases availability.
3. **STRUCTURAL THREATS:** When the structure of a business has a failure. For example, if a company's power went out causing a decrease in availability.
4. **ENVIRONMENTAL THREATS:** These include disasters that are outside of the control of the company. These could include things such as terrorist attacks or natural disasters.

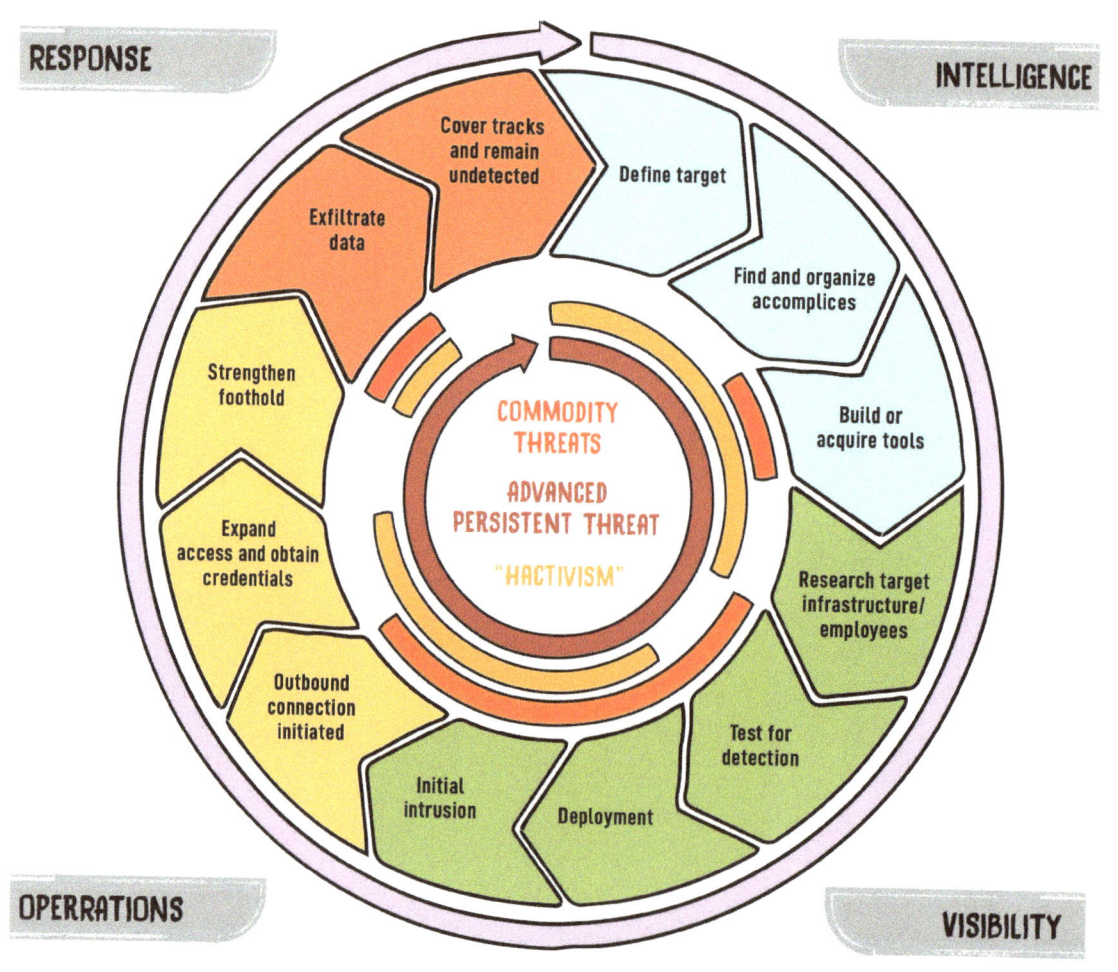

## RISK

To understand risk, first we must understand the terms asset, vulnerability, and threat.

Firstly, all risk happens on an asset. An asset is anything an entity has of value. Assets can include things like hardware, software, and information. If something can be lost, stolen, or damaged and thus negatively impact an organization, that something would be an asset.

Secondly, risk can only occur when there is a vulnerability. A vulnerability is any system defect that can lead to an entity being harmed. Finally, a threat is anything that can exploit a vulnerability. To summarize with an example, if there is a bug in a company's network configurations that could lead to a hacker infiltrating the network, that bug would be a vulnerability and the hackers would be a threat. So then, risk is when an asset has a vulnerability that intersects with a threat. Risk reflects the probability that a threat would cause harm.

$$\text{RISK} = \text{THREAT} \times \text{VULNERABILITY} \times \text{IMPACT}$$

This simply means that risk is determined where a threat, vulnerability, and impact intersect.

## RISK EVALUATION

Risk evaluation is comprised of two questions:

1. How likely is it that a threat will create a risk? In other words, what is the probability that a threat and vulnerability will overlap? This is called likelihood.
2. If there is a risk, what is the probability that it will cause harm? This is called impact.

Let's first consider likelihood.

If you were to run a website that only shows pictures of dogs and never stores any sensitive information, there would not be a high probability that risk would occur. Even if there was a vulnerability in the way your website was set up, there would not be an incentive for a threat to exploit this vulnerability. In this situation, you would have low risk.

However, if you ran a website with credit card information on the backend and had the same vulnerability as the dog picture website, your risk would be higher. The probability that a threat might try to exploit the vulnerability would be raised, because the incentive for a hacker in this scenario is greater.

Now, let's consider the impact.

Again, imagine that you own a website which stores sensitive credit card information on the backend and that your website is vulnerable.

If a threat can occur but the impact isn't too large, this vulnerability may not add a lot of risk. For instance, if a hacker infiltrates the system by using a vulnerability, but all information within the database is encrypted, the hacker might not be able to cause any harm to the organization.

On the other hand, if all data is in plaintext and the hacker is able to access sensitive information, this would represent a higher impact, and thus a higher risk.

When evaluating a risk, both the likelihood and impact must be taken into consideration.

## ASSESSING RISK

There are two types of risk assessments, qualitative and quantitative.

Quantitative risks are those that can be represented with numbers. An example of a quantitative risk can be seen in Annual Loss Expectancy (ALE), which is comprised of Single Loss Expectancy (SLE) and the Annual Rate of Occurrence (ARO).

$$ALE = SLE \times ARO$$

For example, if something happens once every ten years, the occurrences would be 0.1 times per year. If the cost of that event is $500,000, then the ALE would be calculated:

$$ALE = \$500,000 \times .01 \quad => \quad ALE = \$50,000$$

When performing quantitative risk assessment, the ALE is used to determine how much money should be spent on managing the risk. In the case of the above example, it would not make sense to spend over $50,000 a year on a solution which mitigates or transfers that risk.

Qualitative risks are risks that cannot be represented with numbers, but can be given a score. Both likelihood and impact can be evaluated in a qualitative way. These can be given values such as 'high', 'medium', or 'low'; you could say that a risk has a 'low' likelihood of occurring or a 'high' likelihood of occurring. Because this is qualitative, there is not an exact formula for how this is calculated, and judgement is needed to determine the risk of an event's likelihood or impact.

## MANAGING RISK

There are four main types of risk management.

1. **RISK AVOIDANCE:** When an organization takes action to avoid risks. For example, when an organization stops using an old operating system due to vulnerabilities, that's risk avoidance.

2. **RISK ACCEPTANCE:** Also known as Risk Tolerance, this is when an organization simply accepts a risk. An organization may accept a risk if the cost of removing the vulnerability associated with the risk is very high, but the cost associated with the impact of that risk causing harm is very low.

    Here is a fictional account to illustrate this principle: if an organization finds that it has a vulnerability that could allow a threat agent to steal some intellectual property valued at $100,000, but the cost to fix that vulnerability would be $1,000,000, the organization may choose to not fix the vulnerability and just accept the risk.

3. **RISK MITIGATION:** When an organization reduces risk. When a risk is mitigated, it is not completely removed or avoided, it is simply reduced. One example is when companies provide training to teach their employees about phishing scams. This mitigates the risk that an employee will give out his or her credentials to someone else, but does not avoid it altogether. In other words, it reduces the likelihood that an employee would give someone unauthorized access to a system, but it does not eliminate it altogether.

4. **RISK TRANSFERENCE:** This involves shifting the risk to another party. A classic example of risk transference is insurance. People and companies often pay for insurance policies, and in turn, insurance companies take on risk.

There are two main types of controls that are used to manage risk.

1. **TECHNICAL CONTROLS:** These are hardware and software controls that companies can use to manage risk, such as firewalls and intrusion detection systems.

2. **OPERATION CONTROLS:** These are things such as hiring practices and physical security protocols that provide guidelines to increase an organization's security.

## NON-TECHNICAL SOURCES OF RISK

When most people think about risk in terms of cybersecurity, it's easy to think of all threats as hackers trying to get into systems by taking advantage of technical vulnerabilities. However, this isn't always the case. Some attackers use social engineering.

Social engineering occurs when an attacker manipulates someone into divulging information or committing an action. For instance, a person who lacks access to a server room may attempt to socially engineer their way in by telling a guard they forgot their badge at home.

One other non-technical source of risk is phishing. Phishing is an attempt to obtain sensitive information by disguising an electronic communication to make it look as though it came from a trusted source. So, an attacker could first gather a bunch of company emails through email harvesting. Once the attacker has the list of email addresses, he/she could send out emails to company employees and ask them to reset their password. The attacker could make the email and the password reset page look official by using the company's logo and other means to trick the employees into entering their passwords into an insecure input box.

# VULNERABILITY MANAGEMENT: PROCESSES & SCANNING

# INFORMATION SECURITY VULNERABILITY MANAGEMENT PROCESS

## REGULATORY ENVIRONMENTS

Companies that deal with sensitive information may fall under a regulatory environment. Some regulatory environments have laws that specifically state how certain assets should be handled.

One example of this is HIPAA, which stands for Health Insurance Portability & Accountability Act. HIPAA regulates the way that any entity dealing with health data should handle that data.

Another is GLBA (Gramm-Leach-Bliley Act), which dictates how financial institutions handle data.

HIPAA and GLBA do not specify how vulnerability management programs should be implemented. There are more in depth schemes that do specify an implementation.

One example of this is FISMA (the Federal Information Security Management Act). FISMA applies to government agencies to ensure that they employ specific controls depending on how critical it is for their systems to maintain confidentiality, integrity, and availability.

Another regulatory environment is PCI DSS (Payment Card Industry Data Security Standard). This is a standard, not a law, maintained by the Payment Card Industry Security Standards Council. This includes how often organizations must run vulnerability scans, who may conduct them, and how discovered vulnerabilities should be resolved. Self-imposed regulations promote a culture of security, preventing unnecessary governmental regulation.

## CORPORATE POLICY

Companies might develop their own policy for how to manage vulnerabilities if its concerns differ from the industry as a whole. Many companies' vulnerability management strategies are inherited from their chosen IT governance framework (i.e. COBIT, ITIL, ISO 27000, CMMI, etc.).

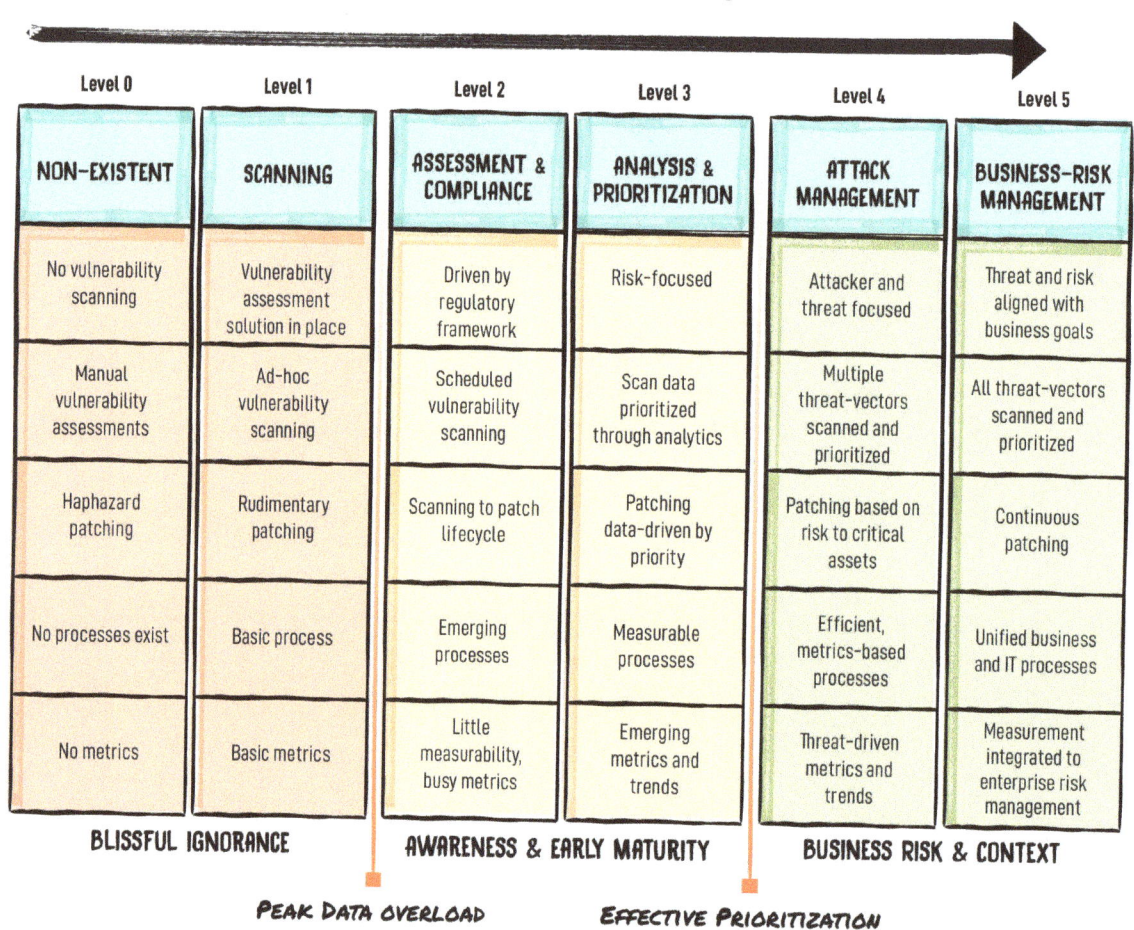

Governance frameworks typically outline policies that address major components of vulnerability management: identification, categorization, and remediation. Like any corporate policy, support and enforcement from upper management are key to the success of vulnerability management.

# DATA CLASSIFICATION

This is an important step in determining a corporate policy. Data classification involves two main steps: identifying information, and assigning value to information. Data classification can be used to create an asset inventory, which lists anything of value to the company. The asset inventory should categorize assets as critical or non-critical depending on how the loss of those assets could affect integrity, confidentiality or availability.

A well-maintained asset inventory helps security professionals determine which vulnerability assessments are necessary, how often they should be performed, and which assets to assess.

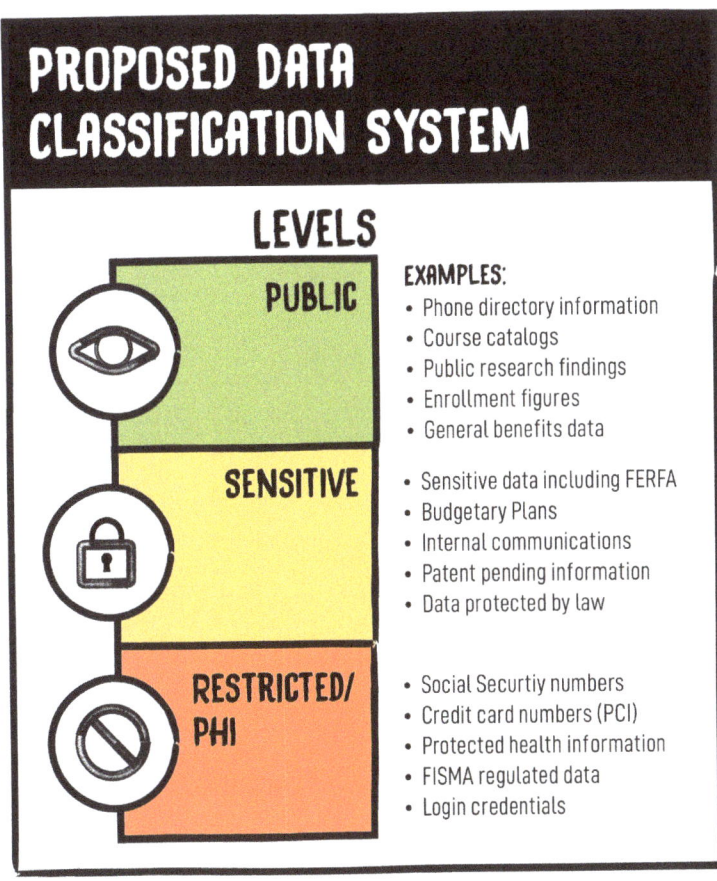

# ESTABLISH SCANNING FREQUENCY

Many vulnerability scanners can be set to automatically scan a network at certain times. For example, a company could set up a Nessus vulnerability scanner to scan their network every Tuesday at 8AM and send a report to an administrator. Whether automation is available or not, a security professional must be able to answer the question, "How often should scanning take place?" There are four things to consider when answering this question.

**RISK APPETITE:** Risk appetite is an organization's willingness to take on risk. So an organization with a high risk appetite might choose to scan less often.

**REGULATORY REQUIREMENTS:** Regulations, like FISMA, sometimes state how often a network should be scanned. These regulations establish a maximum allowable interval between scans.

**TECHNICAL CONSTRAINTS:** Technical constraints must be taken into account when deciding on scanning frequency. The size of the network or limitations of the scanning tool may limit the system to one thorough scan per day.

**WORKFLOW:** Vulnerability scans consume computer resources. Limiting the number of scans run during peak business hours will help avoid bogging down the system.

## FURTHER CONFIGURATION OF VULNERABILITY SCANNERS

Vulnerability scanners have many configurable attributes in addition to frequency. A security professional should be aware of these options and how they affect a vulnerability scan. A selection of these options are discussed below.

## SCANNING CRITERIA & SENSITIVITY LEVELS

Vulnerability scanners can be configured to limit searches to specific machines and operating systems. For example, Nessus vulnerability scanners come with plug-ins that allow modular management of scanner activity. These modules can be enabled or disabled as needed.

For example, some modules available in a Nessus vulnerability scanner include searching for known backdoors, common misconfiguration, local security checks, and more. With a tool like this, information security professionals can specify which OS's to include / exclude in a scan.

For highly sensitive systems the scanner can be configured to omit certain actions in order to reduce the risk of harming a system unnecessarily.

## VULNERABILITY FEED

New vulnerabilities are discovered all the time. A vulnerability feed is one way for cybersecurity professionals to remain aware of all of the vulnerabilities that may impact his or her network. A vulnerability feed lists all vulnerabilities in a category, and can be automatically retrieved by vulnerability scanners so that the scanners test for the most up-to-date set of vulnerabilities. https://nvd.nist.gov/vuln/data-feeds is a website that contains some vulnerability feeds.

## SCOPE

The scope of a vulnerability scan answers the question, "What assets are being scanned and how aggressively?" It is important to strike a balance with the scope of a test. When the scope is too narrow, vulnerabilities on critical assets may go unnoticed. If the scope is too broad or aggressive, it could consume unnecessary bandwidth on the network or cause problems in certain systems.

## CREDENTIALED VS. NON-CREDENTIALED

In a credentialed scan, the vulnerability scanner has access to all internal systems. This provides for a more invasive scan.

In a non-credentialed scan, the vulnerability scanner employs no credentials. A non-credentialed scan operates "from the outside" as though initiated by an attacker. In this way, it can reveal to a security professional what would be discoverable during an attack.

Both types of scans reveal important information to a security professional. Some security professionals argue that non-credentialed scans yield higher priority vulnerabilities because attackers without any system access could more easily access the same vulnerabilities.

Credentialed scanning provides greater access to the network than non-credentialed scanning. For instance, a credentialed scan may have access to databases / specific applications on a host.

## SERVER-BASED VS. AGENT-BASED

A server-based scan, in which a server performs the vulnerability scan, is the most traditional form of a vulnerability scan.

In agent-based vulnerability scans, hosts on the network download software associated with the vulnerability scanner. When the server requests a vulnerability report, the hosts scan themselves and send a report to the server.

Agent-based vulnerability scanning provides an advantage since the server does not maintain credentials with access to many different machines.

## TOOL UPDATES / PLUG-INS

As new vulnerabilities are discovered and reported in vulnerability feeds, security professionals must keep vulnerability tools and plug-ins current. Updates are released for tools and plug-ins in response to updates from vulnerability feeds, or even for vulnerabilities discovered within the vulnerability scanners themselves.

## SCAP

Security Content Automation Protocol (SCAP) is a standard made by the security community to ensure that automated vulnerability scanners comply with specific policies. For example, SCAP guidance could ensure that a company's use of a vulnerability scanner complies with FISMA.

## GENERATING REPORTS

Information from a vulnerability scanner is useless if it never reaches administrators who can remediate the issue.

Reports can be distributed to the people who need to view them in different ways.

Manual distribution requires an administrator to sift through all information that a vulnerability scanner produces and distribute the information accordingly.

This approach can be time consuming, so there is also an option for reports to be automatically sent to those who need to see them. Vulnerability scanners can be configured to deliver reports to administrators at certain time intervals, or if certain critical vulnerabilities are discovered.

## TYPES OF FINDINGS

When reports are generated, they produce findings which must be acted upon in order to keep the environment secure. When reviewing the report, an engineer may run into findings which are not really security issues, these are called false positives. Anytime a report is reviewed, it is important to consider the different types of findings, and non-findings, as seen below:

**FALSE POSITIVE:** When a vulnerability is detected where none exists
**FALSE NEGATIVE:** When a vulnerability is not detected
**TRUE POSITIVE:** When a vulnerability is correctly detected
**TRUE NEGATIVE:** When a vulnerability is not detected and does not exist

Ideally, we want all of our scans to produce true positives and true negatives, as false positives and false negatives create additional overhead during mitigation. This may require fine tuning the scanning devices that are used within the environment. Behavior-based scanning, in general, can produce many false findings if not properly configured.

# REMEDIATION

Being aware of a vulnerability is only half the battle. A security professional must then remediate the threat by either removing the vulnerability, or managing the impact it might have.

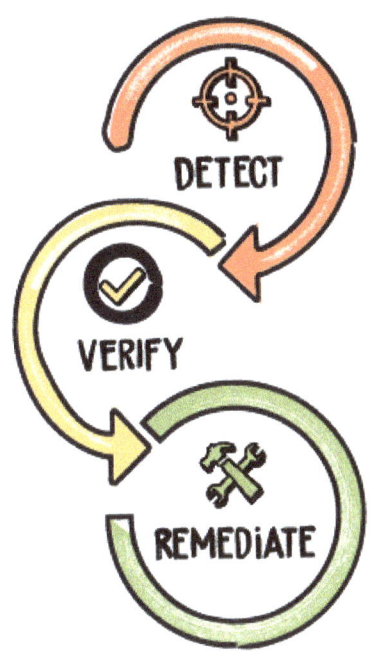

Remediation follows detection, as shown in the vulnerability management lifecycle below.

Detection is the action or process by which a cybersecurity professional becomes aware of a vulnerability, such as a running vulnerability scan. Remediation is the security professional's response to detection. Verification, or testing, concerns ensuring that the remediation worked.

The following concepts will be helpful as you consider remediation options for a detected vulnerability.

**PRIORITIZING:** This is a key concern of remediation. Though it would be nice to fix all vulnerabilities, companies may have limited resources. Additionally, remediating one vulnerability could have unexpected, undesirable consequences. Consider the following when prioritizing the remediation of different vulnerabilities.

**CRITICALITY:** Refers to how much the vulnerability could affect integrity, confidentiality, and availability if it were to be exploited. If all of these are high, the vulnerability would be highly critical.

**DIFFICULTY OF IMPLEMENTATION:** Not all vulnerabilities have the same difficulty to remediate. Remediating some vulnerabilities may simply require that an unused port is closed on a system, while others may require a completely different implementation of some software. Given a sample of vulnerabilities of equal criticality, those vulnerabilities that are easiest to remediate should be prioritized.

**BUSINESS PROCESS INTERRUPTION:** Cybersecurity doesn't happen in a vacuum. In determining which vulnerabilities should be remediated and when, consider how remediation will affect normal business processes, particularly if Service Level Agreements (SLAs) are involved.

**SANDBOXING / TESTING:** The practice of taking an application out of the network so that it can be tested. This is often done as part of a remediation technique. Attempting a remediation solution in a sandbox environment provides a risk minimization benefit. Unintended / unexpected consequences of remediation are confined to the sandbox and do not affect the live environment.

**MOUS & SLAS:** Before a security professional begins to remediate a vulnerability, it is important to consult the standing agreements with other branches within the organization, and with outside customers and vendors. Memorandum of Understanding (MOUs) and Service Level Agreements (SLAs) should always be consulted before removing a service or changing a service to remediate a vulnerability.

It is also a good practice for MOUs and SLAs to include verbiage notifying customers of the potential for changes to performance that could occur with vulnerability scans or the remediation of vulnerabilities.

**ORGANIZATIONAL GOVERNANCE:** Cybersecurity concerns go beyond the organization. Bureaucratic obstacles might exist which interfere with remediating a vulnerability. In general, organizational governance processes should be followed when remediating a vulnerability.

**DEGRADING FUNCTIONALITY:** Remember that vulnerability scans consume bandwidth. Some scanners come with settings that allow users to adjust a scan to be more or less aggressive. Scans can also be scheduled for non-peak business hours to minimize degradation in the services' functionality.

Degrading functionality should also be taken into account when deciding how to remediate an issue. For instance, remediating a vulnerability by taking a heavily used web server offline, thus making a business inaccessible to its customers, might be considered a poor remediation tactic.

# ANALYZING VULNERABILITY SCANS: REPORTS

## ANALYZING REPORTS

Vulnerability scan reports can inform the decisions that a security professional makes while identifying and responding to threats. Familiarizing yourself with the structure of your reports will help you interpret scan results and take the most appropriate action.

Consider the following Nessus report:

Report generated by Nessus™

Uncredentialed Windows 2003 Network Scan, Vulnerabilities by Plugin
Mon, 11 Dec 2017 11:45:19 Eastern Standard Time

**TABLE OF CONTENTS**

Hosts Executive Summary
- 192.168.1.128

Hosts Executive Summary                                    Collapse All | Expand All

### 192.168.1.128

| 4 | 0 | 2 | 0 | 28 |
|---|---|---|---|----|
| CRITICAL | HIGH | MEDIUM | LOW | INFO |

| Severity | CVSS | Plugin | Name |
|---|---|---|---|
| CRITICAL | 10.0 | 84729 | Microsoft Windows Server 2003 Unsupported Installation Detection |
| CRITICAL | 10.0 | 97833 | MS17-010: Security Update for Microsoft Windows SMB Server (4013389) (ETERNALBLUE) (ETERNALCHAMPION) (ETERNALROMANCE) (ETERNALSYNERGY) (WannaCry) (EternalRocks) (Petya) (uncredentialed check) |
| CRITICAL | 10.0 | 97994 | Microsoft IIS 6.0 Unsupported Version Detection |
| CRITICAL | 10.0 | 100464 | Microsoft Windows SMBv1 Multiple Vulnerabilities |
| MEDIUM | 6.8 | 90510 | MS16-047: Security Update for SAM and LSAD Remote Protocols (3148527) (Badlock) (uncredentialed check) |
| MEDIUM | 5.0 | 57608 | SMB Signing Disabled |
| INFO | N/A | 10107 | HTTP Server Type and Version |
| INFO | N/A | 10114 | ICMP Timestamp Request Remote Date Disclosure |
| INFO | N/A | 10150 | Windows NetBIOS / SMB Remote Host Information Disclosure |
| INFO | N/A | 10287 | Traceroute Information |
| INFO | N/A | 10394 | Microsoft Windows SMB Log In Possible |

As it says in the top left corner, this was an uncredentialed scan, meaning that the scanner did not have any usernames / passwords to scan machines more thoroughly.

Below is the Hosts Executive Summary. Here, the vulnerability scanner has organized its findings by criticality, with red representing the most critical threats and blue indicating least critical.

Each of the findings is labeled with the color-coded Severity level, the CVSS score, the Plugin ID, and the name of the vulnerability detected.

CVSS stands for "Common Vulnerability Scoring System". The CVSS scores, which represent the severity of known vulnerabilities, allow vulnerabilities to be prioritized quickly.

The Plugin ID corresponds with information about that vulnerability. If you were to click on the Plugin ID in the fourth row of the sample report above, further information about that vulnerability would be presented. Here is the output for Plugin ID 100464:

## Microsoft Windows SMBv1 Multiple Vulnerabilities

**CRITICAL**  Nessus Plugin ID 100464

### Synopsis
The remote Windows host is affected by multiple vulnerabilities.

### Description
The remote Windows host has Microsoft Server Message Block 1.0 (SMBv1) enabled. It is, therefore, affected by multiple vulnerabilities :

- Multiple information disclosure vulnerabilities exist in Microsoft Server Message Block 1.0 (SMBv1) due to improper handling of SMBv1 packets. An unauthenticated, remote attacker can exploit these vulnerabilities, via a specially crafted SMBv1 packet, to disclose sensitive information. (CVE-2017-0267, CVE-2017-0268, CVE-2017-0270, CVE-2017-0271, CVE-2017-0274, CVE-2017-0275, CVE-2017-0276)

- Multiple denial of service vulnerabilities exist in Microsoft Server Message Block 1.0 (SMBv1) due to improper handling of requests. An unauthenticated, remote attacker can exploit these vulnerabilities, via a specially crafted SMB request, to cause the system to stop responding. (CVE-2017-0269, CVE-2017-0273, CVE-2017-0280)

- Multiple remote code execution vulnerabilities exist in Microsoft Server Message Block 1.0 (SMBv1) due to improper handling of SMBv1 packets. An unauthenticated, remote attacker can exploit these vulnerabilities, via a specially crafted SMBv1 packet, to execute arbitrary code. (CVE-2017-0272, CVE-2017-0277, CVE-2017-0278, CVE-2017-0279)

Depending on the host's security policy configuration, this plugin cannot always correctly determine if the Windows host is vulnerable if the host is running a later Windows version (i.e., Windows 8.1, 10, 2012, 2012 R2, and 2016) specifically that named pipes and shares are allowed to be accessed remotely and anonymously. Tenable does not recommend this configuration, and the hosts should be checked locally for patches with one of the following plugins, depending on the Windows version : 100054, 100055, 100057, 100059, 100060, or 100061.

### Solution
Apply the applicable security update for your Windows version :

- Windows Server 2008 : KB4018466
- Windows 7 : KB4019264
- Windows Server 2008 R2 : KB4019264
- Windows Server 2012 : KB4019216
- Windows 8.1 / RT 8.1 : KB4019215
- Windows Server 2012 R2 : KB4019215
- Windows 10 : KB4019474
- Windows 10 Version 1511 : KB4019473
- Windows 10 Version 1607 : KB4019472
- Windows 10 Version 1703 : KB4016871
- Windows Server 2016 : KB4019472

### Plugin Details
**Severity:** Critical
**ID:** 100464
**File Name:** ms17_may_smbv1.nasl
**Version:** $Revision: 1.2 $
**Type:** remote
**Agent:** windows
**Family:** Windows
**Published:** 2017/05/26
**Modified:** 2017/08/15
**Dependencies:** 11936, 96982

### Risk Information
**Risk Factor:** Critical

CVSSv2
**Base Score:** 10
**Temporal Score:** 7.4
**Vector:** CVSS2#AV:N/AC:L/Au:N/C:C/I:C/A:C
**Temporal Vector:** CVSS2#E:U/RL:OF/RC:C

CVSSv3
**Base Score:** 9.8
**Temporal Score:** 8.5
**Vector:** CVSS:3.0/AV:N/AC:L/PR:N/UI:N/S:U/C:H/I:H/A:H
**Temporal Vector:** CVSS:3.0/E:U/RL:O/RC:C

### Vulnerability Information
**CPE:** cpe:/o:microsoft:windows
**Required KB Items:** Host/OS, SMB/SMBv1_is_supported
**Exploit Available:** false
**Exploit Ease:** No known exploits are available
**Patch Publication Date:** 2017/05/09
**Vulnerability Publication Date:** 2017/05/09

So the Plugin ID links to a description of and known solutions for the associated vulnerability.

It is worth reiterating the importance of prudence in remediating any vulnerability. A security professional should consider whether updates could cause a degradation of service or violate terms in a service agreement.

If there is uncertainty about how remediation might affect a system, it is best to sandbox the update to determine whether it will produce unintended consequences.

Credentialed and uncredentialed reports are visually similar in that they use the same layout, color schemes, etc. Since a credentialed scan has more complete access to a system, it is likely to report a greater number of vulnerabilities than an uncredentialed scan on the same system.

Here is an example of a credentialed report:

**192.168.1.85**

| CRITICAL | HIGH | MEDIUM | LOW | INFO |
|---|---|---|---|---|
| 12 | 37 | 32 | 4 | 35 |

| Severity | CVSS | Plugin | Name |
|---|---|---|---|
| CRITICAL | 10.0 | 14657 | Red Hat Update Level |
| CRITICAL | 10.0 | 90668 | RHEL 6 : java-1.7.0-openjdk (RHSA-2016:0675) |
| CRITICAL | 10.0 | 91034 | RHEL 5 / 6 / 7 : java-1.6.0-openjdk (RHSA-2016:0723) |
| CRITICAL | 10.0 | 91037 | RHEL 6 : openssl (RHSA-2016:0996) |
| CRITICAL | 10.0 | 91802 | RHEL 6 / 7 : libxml2 (RHSA-2016:1292) |
| CRITICAL | 10.0 | 96403 | RHEL 6 : kernel (RHSA-2017:0036) |
| CRITICAL | 10.0 | 96756 | RHEL 6 : mysql (RHSA-2017:0184) |
| CRITICAL | 10.0 | 97373 | RHEL 6 : kernel (RHSA-2017:0307) |
| CRITICAL | 10.0 | 100400 | RHEL 6 / 7 : samba (RHSA-2017:1270) (SambaCry) |
| CRITICAL | 10.0 | 100401 | RHEL 6 : samba4 (RHSA-2017:1271) (SambaCry) |
| CRITICAL | 10.0 | 101386 | RHEL 6 : kernel (RHSA-2017:1723) |
| CRITICAL | 10.0 | 104843 | RHEL 6 : samba4 (RHSA-2017:3278) |
| HIGH | 9.3 | 92604 | RHEL 5 / 6 / 7 : java-1.7.0-openjdk (RHSA-2016:1504) |
| HIGH | 9.3 | 94623 | RHEL 5 / 6 / 7 : java-1.7.0-openjdk (RHSA-2016:2658) |
| HIGH | 9.3 | 94912 | RHEL 5 / 6 / 7 : nss and nss-util (RHSA-2016:2779) |

## FALSE POSITIVES & EXCEPTIONS

While scanners provide useful information, their output is not always accurate. When a vulnerability scanner identifies something innocuous as a vulnerability, it is said to have returned a "false positive".

Best practice is to always confirm that a vulnerability exists prior to remediating it. Confirmation is sometimes as straightforward as verifying that an update has not been installed. In other instances, confirmation requires much more effort. For instance, a security professional would need to test a reported SQL injection vulnerability by attempting SQL injection.

Remember that the goal of a cybersecurity professional is not always to eliminate risk, but to manage it with deference to the CIA triad. A vulnerability might prove too expensive to fix when considering the harm that remediation might cause the company. In such a case, a cybersecurity professional might add this vulnerability as an exception in the vulnerability scanner. This avoids constant reporting on issues already known to administrators.

# ANALYZING VULNERABILITY SCANS: CORRELATION

## RELATED LOGS & RECONCILING RESULTS

When examining vulnerability scan results, consider information that can be gained from other network devices. These include logs from network devices, SIEM systems, and configuration management systems. Cybersecurity professionals can use this information to improve their understanding of vulnerabilities on the network.

For example, if a vulnerability scanner shows that a known vulnerability exists on the network, it would be prudent to check the logs and ensure that the vulnerability has not yet been exploited.

Specifically, if a vulnerability scanner showed a Server Message Block (SMB) vulnerability in the network, a cybersecurity professional should examine the logs for suspicious traffic on port 445 since it correlates with SMB.

## DETERMINE TRENDS

Vulnerability scanners can also be used to gather analytics on trends in network traffic. The following report provides a variety of vulnerability trend analyses.

## BEST PRACTICES

In addition to correlating reported vulnerabilities with information from network devices, a cybersecurity professional should reference industry best practices related to the vulnerability. This means comparing the results of a vulnerability scan with information and guidelines from a trusted source. Modern vulnerability scanners incorporate best practices as a part of reporting.

For instance, the Nessus vulnerability scanner assigns a severity description (low, medium, high, or critical) to each vulnerability based on its CVSS score. Those two things together are a way to compare configurations (the descriptor) with best practice guidelines (CVSS score).

Vulnerability scanners might also provide information regarding best practices for remediating vulnerabilities. For example, the output above that showed the information about the SMBv1 vulnerabilities gave information from Nessus about the best practice to remove this vulnerability.

# VULNERABILITY MANAGEMENT: COMMON VULNERABILITIES

# SERVERS & ENDPOINTS

Modern operating systems running on servers and endpoints within a network provide users with extensive capabilities. These sophisticated capabilities are the product of increased complexity as modern OSs rely on millions of lines of code. With greater complexity comes an increased risk for unintended vulnerabilities.

## MISSING PATCHES

Though simple and avoidable, missing patches are among the most common vulnerabilities. When a vendor, such as Microsoft, discovers a vulnerability in their software they will release a patch. A patch is an update that resolves a vulnerability or some other issue. Missing patches are fixed by installing the vendor-supplied patch.

Vendors might end support for legacy operating systems at some point during that system's lifecycle, meaning the vendor no longer develops patches for vulnerabilities found in the operating system. This happens typically about a decade after the operating system has been released.

The Nessus report below describes an unsupported installation discovered during a scan.

### Microsoft Windows Server 2003 Unsupported Installation Detection

**CRITICAL** Nessus Plugin ID 84729

**Synopsis**
The remote operating system is no longer supported.

**Description**
The remote host is running Microsoft Windows Server 2003. Support for this operating system by Microsoft ended July 14th, 2015.

Lack of support implies that no new security patches for the product will be released by the vendor. As a result, it is likely to contain security vulnerabilities. Furthermore, Microsoft is unlikely to investigate or acknowledge reports of vulnerabilities.

**Solution**
Upgrade to a version of Windows that is currently supported.

**See Also**
http://www.nessus.org/u?c0dbe792
http://www.nessus.org/u?321523eb
https://blogs.technet.microsoft.com/filecab/2016/09/16/stop-using-smb1/
http://www.nessus.org/u?8dcab5e4

**Plugin Details**
**Severity:** Critical
**ID:** 84729
**File Name:** smb_win_2003.nasl
**Version:** $Revision: 1.8 $
**Type:** combined
**Agent:** windows
**Family:** Windows
**Published:** 2015/07/14
**Modified:** 2017/11/21
**Dependencies:** 11936

**Risk Information**
**Risk Factor:** Critical

**CVSSv2**
**Base Score:** 10
**Temporal Score:** 8.3
**Vector:** CVSS2#AV:N/AC:L/Au:N/C:C/I:C/A:C

An unsupported OS receives a CVSS score of 10, meaning that remediation is a critical necessity. Notice under "Description" that the report does not list specific vulnerabilities in the operating system, but merely states that it is likely to contain vulnerabilities. Notice also under "Solution" that no patches are recommended. Rather, the recommendation is to switch to a supported OS.

## BUFFER OVERFLOWS

The operating system, along with a program running on that OS, determines how memory is allocated physically in a machine. As a result, sensitive data could occasionally be stored near input data in a computer's architecture.

Imagine a computer program that allocates 32 bytes for the collection of a user's name. What if a user entered 40 bytes of data into the box for his or her name? The extra 8 bytes might be written in the location directly following the input box in the computer's memory. This would be a buffer overflow. While software development methods exist to protect against these buffer overflows, such a discussion is beyond the scope of this book. However, a cybersecurity professional should understand the concept of buffer overflow. Buffer overflow occurs when more data is written into a buffer than intended, and the additional data overflows into other parts of memory.

## ARBITRARY CODE EXECUTION

Arbitrary code execution vulnerabilities allow a user to execute software on a system despite the user's permissions. This vulnerability is critical as it allows an attacker to introduce and run any code, including additional exploits, on a system.

## INSECURE PROTOCOL USE

Archaic internet protocols were not designed with built-in security. Telnet, TCP port 23, is an example of such a protocol.

Telnet, developed in 1969, allows a user to log into a terminal remotely and does not encrypt any traffic it sends. Usernames and passwords transmitted via Telnet could be captured in Wireshark by anyone listening on the network. It is important to use secure protocols.

In contrast to Telnet, SSH supports encryption by default. For this reason, SSH is preferred when connecting to a remote terminal.

Examples of other insecure protocols include:

- TCP 21 : File Transfer Protocol (FTP)
- TCP 25 : Simple Mail Transfer Protocol (SMTP)
- TCP 80 : HyperText Transfer Protocol (HTTP)
- TCP 110 : Post Office Protocol 3 (POP3)
- TCP & UDP 135 : Microsoft Remote Procedure Call (RPC)
- TCP 143 : Internet Message Access Protocol (IMAP)

## SQL INJECTION

SQL (Structured Query Language) is a language used to access and alter backend databases. SQL databases are commonly encountered and used for storing information on a network.

An injection attack submits code through an input box. This code circumvents access controls and is executed in the backend environment.

For instance, imagine that an input box on a web page asks a user for his or her favorite animal, and any text entered in is processed by an SQL command and input to the database. However, what would happen if an attacker entered an SQL command instead of an animal name? On an unprotected site, the submitted SQL command would be executed in the backend environment. As this circumvents access controls, the attacker is able to access privileged information like usernames and passwords and even destroy the database entirely.

## TYPES OF SQL ATTACKS

**STANDARD SQL INJECTION:** SQL query commands are input into an application, using it as an interface into the backend database. The commands injected into the application can be used to access information or tamper with the database itself. Frequently, the error messages that the server returns provide the attacker with information, aiding their efforts.

**BLIND SQL INJECTION:** This is the same as standard, with the exception that the attacker receives generic error messages or no error message at all. This forces the attacker to resort to simple true/false SQL query operations to extract information from the system, as they are not presented with detailed information on the success (or failure) of their commands.

**OUT-OF-BAND SQL INJECTION:** This relies on DNS and HTTP queries to deliver the injection attack, rather than an application interfacing directly with the database. This attack requires the database server to have certain features enabled that are vulnerable to such delivery methods.

**COMPOUND SQL INJECTION:** This is the act of combining SQLi with other attack methods. Such additional attacks can include: DoS, DNS hijacking, and cross site scripting. When used together, they can create extremely powerful attacks.

## XSS

In Cross-Site Scripting (XSS), an attacker injects or embeds a script into a webpage so that it will run on computers that visit that website. For example, a user could submit JavaScript through a comment box on a blog. If the website is vulnerable to XSS, then this JavaScript will become part of the page served whenever someone visits the site.

## VIRTUAL INFRASTRUCTURE

Virtualization has grown a lot in popularity lately because it allows teams to use one physical machine to host multiple VMs (virtual machines), which can reduce cost and increase hardware utilization. However, along with these capabilities come some potential problems.

## VIRTUAL HOSTS

Virtual hosts are no different than a physical workstation. They can run outdated and insecure software and must be patched, monitored, and maintained.

A "VM escape" is an attack unique to virtual hosts in which an attacker accesses the host operating system that is running the virtualization software (hypervisor). A successful VM escape provides an attacker with access to the hypervisor and other virtual hosts running on the same machine.

## VIRTUAL NETWORKS

Virtual networks are used to route traffic between virtual hosts no differently than any physical router or firewall, and still require secure practices, such as patching and regular maintenance. Do not mistake a lack of physical network as permission to ignore best practices. Virtual firewalls with good ACLs are as necessary in virtual networks as they are in physical networks.

## VIRTUAL INFRASTRUCTURE MANAGEMENT INTERFACE

The management interface within any kind of virtual infrastructure will have significant power on the network. The management interface sets up new machines and regulates access to resources. A malicious actor who gains control of this could access damaging capabilities on the network. They could deallocate resources to a critical machine, for example.

## NETWORK APPLIANCES & INFRASTRUCTURE

Modern networks are upheld by a variety of networking devices, including routers, firewalls, and switches. Often times these types of devices go unnoticed and unpatched on the network, and might not even show up in your standard vulnerability scan. Patches are usually provided in the form of a firmware update. Firmware is low level software that can interact directly with device hardware. As with software, firmware vulnerabilities are discovered and reported regularly, and vendors will release patches for firmware vulnerabilities.

# MOBILE & INTERCONNECTED NETWORKS

## MOBILE DEVICES

Smart phones, tablets, and other devices can introduce various vulnerabilities into a network. This is an increasing concern for companies that adopt "bring your own device" (BYOD) policies; these devices can be a hazard for confidentiality. If a phone containing sensitive information is not protected with strong passwords and is lost, then confidentiality could be compromised.

Also, like all computing devices, mobile devices have inherent vulnerabilities. Vendors regularly put out patches for known vulnerabilities, so it's best to ensure that these devices are up to date.

Mobile Device Management (MDM) software allows an administrator to manage which phones are allowed access on a company network. This can enforce rules such as having strong passwords and ensuring that mobile devices are completely updated before they are granted network access.

## INTERCONNECTED NETWORKS

Billions of devices connect over the internet, and Internet of Things (IoT) devices account for more and more of those devices each day. Interconnected devices that communicate with each other are broadly referred to as IoT. This includes traditional computing devices, but also smartwatches, smart thermostats, coffee makers, and other everyday devices that support network connectivity.

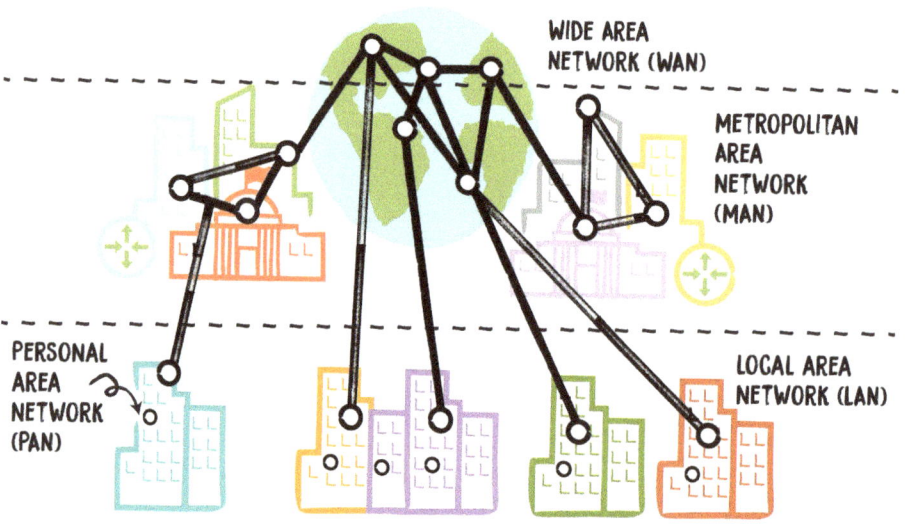

## TYPES OF COMPUTER NETWORKS

These devices can be used as a foothold onto the network. Gaining access to a baby monitor or DVR system on a network might make it easier for an attacker to gain access to more sensitive network devices.

IoT devices could also be used in DDoS attacks. DDoS attacks are distributed denial of service attacks that occur when multiple devices send signals simultaneously to overwhelm an internet service and reduce its availability. These devices are often easily compromised as users often neglect to change credentials from default. IoT devices are enticing targets for attackers who would like to obtain control of many devices in order to perform DDoS attacks.

Another reason to secure IoT devices is that these devices themselves could bring down other systems. For example, consider a network enabled thermostat installed to maintain climate in a server room. An attacker who compromises the network enabled thermostat could cause server failure by increasing the server room temperature beyond safe operation parameters.

# VPNS, ISCS, & SCADA

## VIRTUAL PRIVATE NETWORKS

Virtual private networks (VPNs) extend a private network across a public network. In theory, someone could sit in a coffee shop hundreds of miles away from their office and still operate within the office's private network.

VPN services are not without flaws and vulnerabilities are reported regularly. Patches should be applied as soon as they are available.

Many security issues relating to VPNs stem from using poor or faulty encryption, unpatched software, or weak authentication.

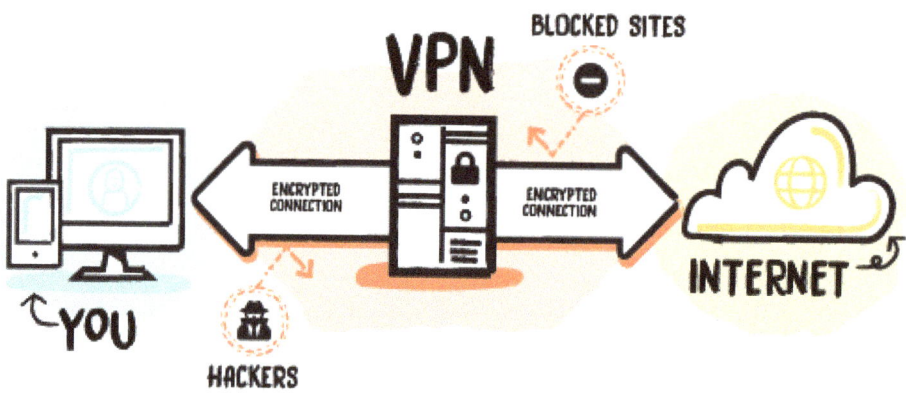

**INSECURE STORAGE OF AUTHENTICATION CREDENTIALS BY VPN CLIENTS:** VPN clients sit on the remote host communicate back to the corporate VPN server. Since remote workers have trusted access into the network, they can become an attractive attack vector for cybercriminals. The VPN client itself can become a viable attack vector when not configured properly. VPN client programs can offer users a faster connection if users store their authentication credentials within the client itself. While this can slightly improve user experience, it also becomes a risk if the client does not implement robust security controls to protect the credentials. A common sense rule of authentication security states that unnecessary storing of credentials increases risk.

**VPN FINGERPRINTING:** Fingerprinting a VPN server can allow an attacker to understand some basic information about the specific VPN implementation being used. Like OS fingerprinting, the information can then be used to see if known vulnerabilities exist for that VPN solution. Attackers then simply use previously revealed exploits to undermine the integrity or confidentiality of the VPN connections and server. This is especially important to consider given that VPN solutions typically sit at the edge of enterprise networks where they can easily be accessed and probed.

## ICSS & SCADA

Industrial control systems monitor and control applications used at electric & power plants, sewage treatment centers, and any building that has an HVAC system. These systems typically receive input from sensors or other control devices and interact with different industrial systems.

SCADA systems have become increasingly relevant security concerns as they now tend to be connected to the internet, making them vulnerable to attack.

A SCADA device should be free of any known vulnerabilities. Patching is key to managing SCADA systems. In addition to patching, traditional tools such as firewalls, and IDSs should be used to secure these systems.

# CYBER INCIDENT RESPONSE

# THREAT CLASSIFICATION

While the intentions of any security strategy are to never have an incident that lowers the confidentiality, integrity, or availability of services, it's prudent to plan for how to deal with a security incident in the event that one occurs. The first step in handling a threat is to define it, so that the proper steps to eradicate or mitigate it can be taken.

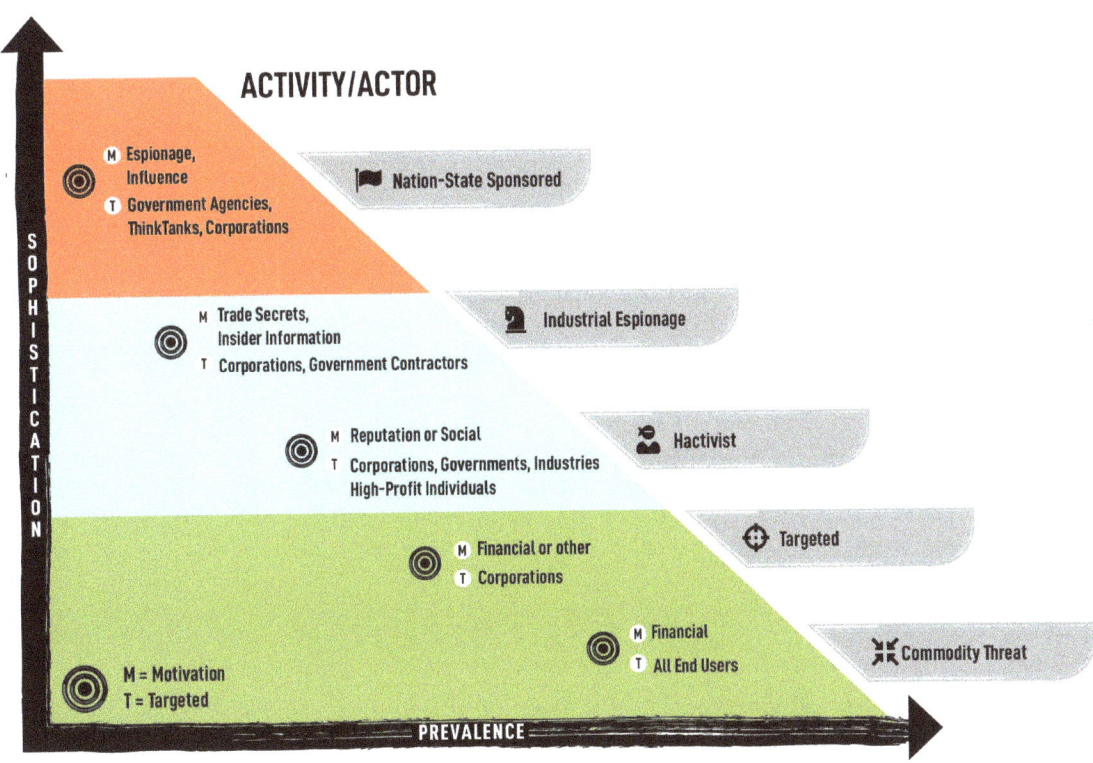

## KNOWN VS. UNKNOWN

Known Threats have been published and the security community is aware of them. For instance, a piece of malware that was discovered a few years prior. Many different organizations make this information available to the public in an effort to educate security professionals and improve the overall posture of global I.T. systems. MITRE assigns most known vulnerabilities with a Common Vulnerabilities and Exposures (CVE) number which other organizations can use as a reference when sharing information on a particular vulnerability. The National Institute of Standards & Technology (NIST) provides the National Vulnerability Database (NVD), where you can research CVEs for more detailed information, such as severity, patching resources, and specifics on which systems are affected.

Because these threats have been in the wild before, detection mechanisms are built into systems such as firewalls, IDSs, and IPSs. These devices can use signature updates to detect and prevent known vulnerabilities from reaching targets within a trusted network that could be exploitable.

Unknown Threats are those that have never been seen in the wild before and as a result, are much harder to identify. In order to detect these, heuristic analysis is needed. Since these threats may not have the same signature as a known threat, it iss important to look at what these pieces of software are doing. Heuristic analysis can detect new threats by comparing programs against known malicious code or sandboxing programs to inspect the outcome.

Note that both known and unknown threats may try to exploit the same vulnerability. Limiting the vulnerabilities in a network by installing patches can reduce the risk of an unknown threat causing harm to confidentiality, integrity, or availability. Scanning for threats at different points within the network (such as both the external firewall and the host) can also assist in limiting the amount of exposure a system has.

## ZERO DAY

A zero day is when a previously unknown vulnerability is exploited. These can be especially hard to defend against, since the vendors who made the software haven't released a patch to protect these vulnerabilities.

One of the best defenses against a zero day is to use behavioral analysis, to analyze exactly what the software is doing.

# ADVANCED PERSISTENT THREAT

An advanced persistent threat is a threat that infiltrates a network and persists for a long period of time, using advanced techniques.

Advanced persistent threats typically target specific entities, such as a business or government, with a specific goal. These may use techniques to infect multiple machines on a network and slowly leak out data, doing their best to remain undetected.

"Advanced persistent threat" is a broad term that doesn't specify the specific means by which an actor comes to be an advanced persistent threat. These threats could gain access to information through known vulnerabilities, zero day attacks, or social engineering.

The important thing to remember about an advanced persistent threat is that its goal is to persist on the network. So, it wouldn't take down servers the moment it gained access to them. These threats have a goal of remaining undetected for long periods of time, perhaps to cause more harm than they could in a short period of time, or to leak out information undetected.

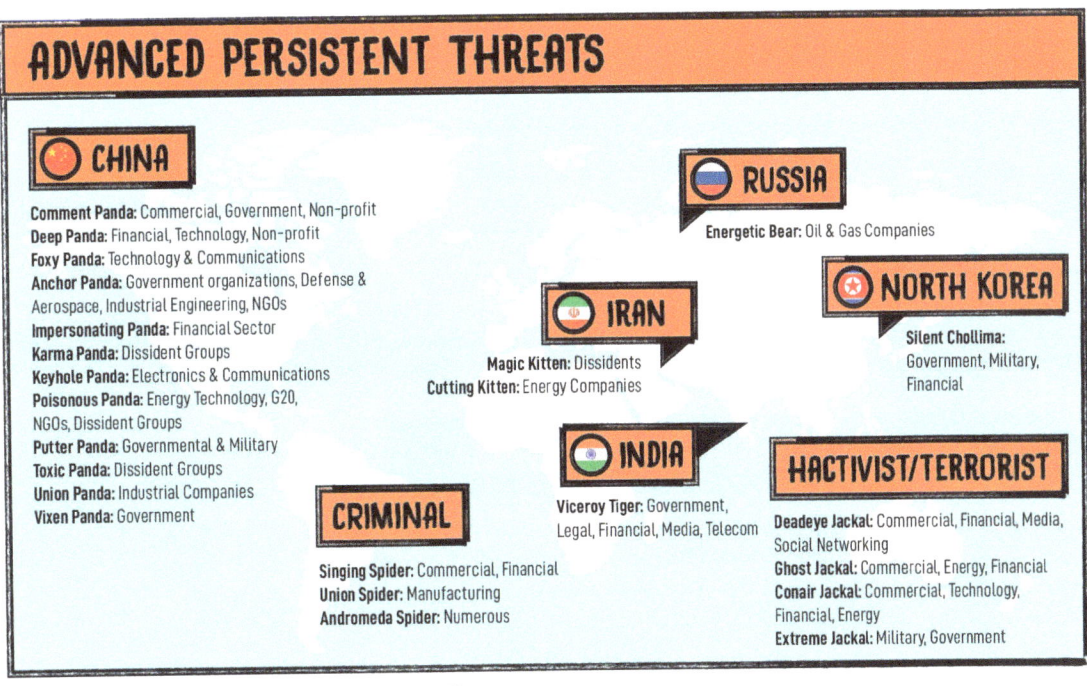

# FACTORS OF DETERMINATION

## INCIDENT SEVERITY & PRIORITIZATION

Not all security incidents are the same; they vary in severity. With some, personal information is stolen and entire systems are brought down, while others are much less serious. Two important factors for measuring severity are the scope of impact and types of data involved. NIST (National Institute of Standards & Technology) has released guidelines that people use to measure severity.

### NIST FUNCTIONAL IMPACT CHART

| | |
|---|---|
| **None** | No effect to the organization's ability to provide all services to all users |
| **Low** | Minimal effect; the organization can still provide all critical services to all users but has lost efficiency |
| **Medium** | Organization has lost the ability to provide a critical service to a subset of system users |
| **High** | Organization is no longer able to provide some critical services to any users |

## DATA INTEGRITY

It's also important to consider how data is altered during an incident. If data is changed or if private information is accessed, this could contribute to how severe the incident is.

### NIST INFORMATION IMPACT CHART

| | |
|---|---|
| **None** | No information was exfiltrated, changed, deleted, or otherwise compromised |
| **Privacy Breach** | Sensitive personally identifiable information (PII) of taxpayers, employees, beneficiaries, etc. was accessed or exfiltrated |
| **Proprietary Breach** | Unclassified proprietary information, such as protected critical infrastructure information (PCII), was accessed or exfiltrated |
| **Integrity Loss** | Sensitive or proprietary information was changed or deleted |

## TYPES OF DATA

Just as not all incidents are equal, not all data breaches are equal. The type of data accessed or released changes the severity of the incident. Below is a chart that shows different types of data with their definitions.

| | Type | Definition |
|---|---|---|
| | **Personally Identifiable Information (PII)** | This is information that can be used on its own to locate, contact, or identify an individual. |
| | **Personal Health Information (PHI)** | This is health information that the government has deemed to be protected, such as diagnosis or medical treatments. |
| | **Payment card information** | This is information relating to a payment card that could be used to make unauthorized purchases in someone else's name. |
| | **Intellectual property** | This is creative property, such as a screenplay, that has some value and is owned by some entity. |
| | **Accounting data** | This is data used to account for the financial status of an entity |
| | **Mergers and acquisitions** | These relate to corporate structural changes in which one or more than one company are absorbed or merge with another. |

# COMMON SYMPTOMS

## NETWORK RELATED

Noticing network-related symptoms help security professionals to spot an attack early, and thus get a jump start on the response. This section will go through some of the common symptoms a network may show if there is a security incident.

**BANDWIDTH CONSUMPTION AND TRAFFIC SPIKES:** While unusual bandwidth consumption could be a concern on its own for network managers, bandwidth consumption can be one of the first signs that a security incident is occurring on the network. One of the best ways to monitor bandwidth is with Netflow Traffic Analyzer.

Netflow Traffic Analyzer is a tool that allows users to visualize bandwidth usage both on a single device and on a network, and can display bandwidth usage in a few different ways. For example, it can show which hosts are using the most traffic, or which applications are using the most traffic.

One common cause of traffic spikes on a network is denial-of-service (DoS) attacks. Denial of service attacks try to bring down the availability of a specific service. Many of these attacks are done by attempting to overwhelm a network by flooding it with connection requests that the service doesn't have time to respond to. This could cause a traffic spike.

**BEACONING:** Often malware is written so if ever installed on a computer, it will send out a signal to a C2 (Command and Control) server. This signal could alert the attacker that a machine has been infected, provide some other status, or request a command. This is known as beaconing.

One of the best ways to detect beaconing is with the use of an IDS or IPS. These use behavioral analysis to detect odd behavior. Information from these devices can be used in conjunction with a packet analyzer to learn what information was sent by the computer in question.

**IRREGULAR PEER-TO-PEER COMMUNICATION:** Unusual peer-to-peer communication can also be a sign of a security incident.

In a peer-to-peer network, each computer can act as both a server and a client. The workload of the network can be distributed among all of the peers. Peer-to-peer network communication is common with file sharing and may be a symptom of a malicious actor attempting to exfiltrate data from the network.

Like other symptoms, IDSs and IPSs can be used to detect irregular peer-to-peer communication. It could use baseline analysis, heuristic analysis, or protocol analysis, which is arguably the best to use in this circumstance.

**ROGUE DEVICES ON THE NETWORK:** An attacker may try to get a device onto a network in order to explore the network or to gain higher rights and privileges. So, it's important to monitor who is and isn't on the network.

The first line of defense against rogues on a network is access control technologies, which limit the devices that are allowed to be on a network to only approved devices.

In case this doesn't work, there are a few ways that security professionals can find rogue devices on a network. One way is to use valid MAC address checking. This is when all MAC addresses on the network are checked against a list of acceptable devices to ensure that no unknown devices are on the network. One very simple way to check for this is to physically survey the site, looking for suspicious devices implanted.

Another way to look for rogue devices is to use network scanning tools, such as NMAP, to look for new devices that aren't authorized to be on the network. In an enterprise network, Wireless LAN Controllers (WLCs) also have functionality built that allows for an AP whitelist, reporting when an unauthorized AP is connected to the network.

**SCAN SWEEPS:** Scanning a network is often one of the first steps that an attacker or a pentester might take if they were doing reconnaissance on a network. These scans are not inherently very damaging to the network by themselves. These scans are a part of the discovery phase for an attacker and are often a precursor to other attacks.

Modern IDSs and IPSs should be able to detect network scans. They can do this by detecting certain patterns. For instance, if an IP address pings each IP address on a network in ascending order, this would be a symptom of a network scan.

## APPLICATION RELATED

Applications can also display various symptoms when attacked, and looking for these behaviors can help in detecting an attack as early as possible. The following covers a variety of different application-related symptoms.

**ANOMALOUS ACTIVITY:** This refers to activity that lies outside the range of normal behaviors for a particular system. Behavioral analysis and log analysis can be used to ensure that an application is behaving normally.

**INTRODUCTION OF NEW ACCOUNTS:** New, unexpected accounts are often a sign of an attack. Attackers will make new accounts as a way of escalating rights and privileges. It's an especially good idea to look for new administrative accounts, as these would be sought after by an attacker.

**UNEXPECTED OUTPUT:** Unexpected output can take many different forms that depend on the application. For some applications, this may come in the form of strange characters printed in a terminal, while in other applications the unexpected output might just come in the form of erroneous output. This is an application specific thing to spot. Just be sure to know that unexpected output is a sign of an attack on an application.

**UNEXPECTED OUTBOUND COMMUNICATION:** Attackers may try to send files out of the network, or set up a device to perform beaconing. Use of heuristic analysis and trend analysis can create a baseline to compare what a node in a network typically connects to.

**SERVICE INTERRUPTION:** This happens when an application isn't performing properly. Service interruptions can be somewhat benign due to something like a bug in the program. However, this isn't always the case. These can also be due to an increase in traffic from a DoS attack.

**MEMORY OVERFLOWS:** Memory overflows can result from issues inherent in an application, or they can have outside causes. For example, a DoS attack could cause a memory overflow. It's important to log system crashes as well as use IDS and IPS systems to get a better idea of when an attack is occurring.

## HOST RELATED

Along with symptoms that can indicate if there has been a security incident with an application or inside of the network, there are also symptoms that can indicate when something is wrong with a host. The following host-related symptoms may be indicative of a security issue.

**PROCESSOR CONSUMPTION:** Just as bandwidth consumption on a network can be telling of a security incident, processor consumption can reveal an incident on a specific post. There are basic tools built into most operating systems that can display CPU utilization. Sudden and unexpected CPU spikes point to processes that weren't previously active. This might just be a routine application starting up, or it could be indicative of a security event. To determine this, more investigative tools are needed.

**MEMORY CONSUMPTION:** Similar to CPU utilization, memory utilization can indicate how much is happening on a specific host. More activity could be occurring in a host for a benign reason, such as a user opening a new application, or it could also be spiking because of a security issue.

Memory and CPU usage are blunt tools that can show a security professional that more processes are / are not active than previously. These don't necessarily indicate security issues, but they do give information that can be investigated further to get the whole picture. In Windows these statistics are observed in Task Manager; in Linux the command "top" provides this information.

**DRIVE CAPACITY CONSUMPTION:** Hard drive consumption could be another indicator that some security incident has occurred. Drive consumption could change if the computer has downloaded some new software or data onto the machine.

Hard drive consumption doesn't necessarily mean that a security issue is going on, it's just something a security professional should be aware of and monitor. Thankfully, most OSs come with built-in resource monitoring tools that make hard drive capacity easy to see.

**UNAUTHORIZED SOFTWARE & MALWARE:** There are many different tools that attackers may want to download onto a machine. These could include software that monitors a network or computer, viruses, or software that sends beacons to a computer outside of the network.

There are a few ways that malware and unauthorized software can be detected or stopped. The most obvious are antimalware and antivirus tools. These can detect malicious software and can stop an installation, or warn a user that the software about to be installed might be malicious.

Other tools that can be used are central management tools, like SCCM. These allow administrators to manage what software is installed on other computers for security purposes.

The third and fourth ways that malware and unauthorized software can be detected / stopped are application blacklisting and application whitelisting. Application blacklisting happens when an administrator lists specific software to prevent them from being downloaded and installed on a system. Application whitelisting is the opposite; this is when only approved software can be installed on a computer.

**UNAUTHORIZED CHANGES & PRIVILEGES:** One of the primary goals of an attacker might be to escalate their rights and privileges within a network. With extra privileges and rights, attackers have can make modifications to a system and/or access classified information.

Fortunately, most SIEM products come with tools that can detect unauthorized access, changes, and privilege use, helping security professionals become aware of attempts at altering privileges.

**DATA EXFILTRATION:** Data exfiltration is when an attacker tries to get data out of a system. This is extremely harmful to confidentiality, especially if the data is sensitive information.

One of the best defenses for data exfiltration is using IDS and IPS systems that can detect data exfiltration and alert an administrator. These can detect abnormal events on a network and send a message to an administrator, asking them to investigate further. It may then be necessary for the administrator to use a packet analyzer to get a better sense of what is going on. Commercial solutions such as Data Loss Prevention (DLP) software can also detect and prevent exfiltration in enterprise environments.

# DETERMINING INCIDENT IMPACT

## SCOPE OF IMPACT

The scope of the impact is dependent upon how much harm it causes an organization. One of the most obvious and easiest measurements of impact is downtime. Other measurements might be loss of revenue, proprietary data, consumer data, or employee PII.

## DOWNTIME

Downtime is the time that a service is unavailable for use. This could be services used by the company itself. For instance, if developers are not able to use their computers to make software, this would be downtime. Downtime also occurs if public facing services are unavailable. So if a customer is not able to log into a website, this would also be downtime. The Maximum Tolerable Downtime (MTD) is a statistic that businesses use to outline how long services can be down before severely impacting operations.

## SYSTEM PROCESS CRITICALITY

Another way to determine the scope of impact is to look at how critical the processes were that were brought down. System process criticality looks at how important a process is to business functions. A single printer that someone uses isn't as critical as the server that hosts the website.

## RECOVERY TIME

Recovery time refers to the amount of time it takes to respond to an incident and get all systems and processes back to normal. This is an important thing to consider when defining severity, as longer downtimes cost money and reduce availability. Businesses use MTD to determine the Recovery Time Objective (RTO), or how quickly service should be restored after going down.

NIST has a chart that can be used to define recovery efforts:

| | |
|---|---|
| Regular | Time to recovery is predictable with existing resources |
| Supplemented | Time to recovery is predictable with additional resources |
| Extended | Time to recovery is unpredictable; additional resources and outside help are needed |
| Not Recoverable | Recovery from the incident is not possible (e.g., sensitive data exfiltrated and posted publicly); launch investigation |

## DATA RECOVERY

When recovering a system or service, it is also important to consider how much of the data must be recovered to restore business operations. The Recovery Point Objective (RPO) is the maximum amount of data loss a business can withstand. This statistic is frequently used in conjunction with RPO when making recovery plans to ensure that the system can be brought back to an acceptable level of functionality.

## ECONOMIC

The economic impact of a security incident is commonly used to measure how severe it is. Economic costs can be incurred from a lot of different sources. For example, if a data breach turns customers away from a company, impacting revenue, this would be calculated into the economic cost of an incident. Also, more obvious costs should be taken into consideration, such as the monetary value of the hours spent getting a network back online. Knowing the economic impact of a loss is necessary when selecting compensating security controls to ensure that a business does not spend more money on mitigating a threat than the possible financial loss that the threat itself would incur.

# FORENSICS TOOLKIT

Computer forensic investigations help determine what incident happened on a computer or a network. These are similar to physical forensic investigations that law enforcement agencies enact after a crime has been committed in that they seek to understand what happened in the past, not tamper with any of the evidence, and get documented evidence ready to be presented. The following section will go through some of the important forensics toolkit components. The individual tools listed are what is generally needed, however any circumstance may require more or less than the tools listed here.

## DIGITAL FORENSICS WORKSTATION

In theory, a good digital forensics workstation, or sandbox, is any workstation that allows a user to capture and analyze the required information in a timely manner. In the real world, this is typically manifested in a powerful computer with plenty of RAM and storage. Digital forensics may require dealing with a large pool of data, so having the computing power to successfully and efficiently handle this much data is important.

## WRITE BLOCKERS

It is important that the investigators not tamper with evidence, either purposefully or accidentally. This could lead to the findings of the investigation being thrown out. In order to prevent evidence from being tampered with, write blockers are often used. Write blockers make it such that the drives storing the data in question can only be read from, and not written to. This way, neither timestamps nor the data itself cann be altered in the investigation process.

## CABLES & DRIVE ADAPTERS

In cybersecurity, professionals often get to use high tech tools and interesting techniques to do their jobs or to investigate incidents in the past. However, none of this is possible until the right cables and drive adapters are in place. For a security professional, the first step to analyzing data is to be able to access it. Having the correct adapters so that information can be shared between a drive and a workstation is essential for this task.

## WIPED REMOVABLE MEDIA

It is also important to have removable media drives that can be used to transfer data from one computer to another. These can include NAS devices, large solid state drives, USB thumb drives, and SATA hard drive. All of these together can make it easier to transfer data from one system to another during a forensics investigation.

## CAMERAS

Cameras are a great way to document the physical state of something during a forensics investigation. These can be used to record things like cord configurations and labels much faster than they could be recorded by hand with pen and paper.

## CRIME TAPE

Crime tape is either yellow or red tape that alerts someone that the area beyond is either part of an active crime scene or should not be tampered with. While this kind of tape doesn't physically stop someone from tampering with evidence, it can alert them that what is behind the tape is part of an ongoing investigation. This could stop accidental tampering.

## TAMPER-PROOF SEALS

Tamper-proof seals are make it clear if someone has tampered with the contents of any sealed container. They can be used on sensitive files to ensure that no one alters or accesses them without leaving evidence of tampering.

## DOCUMENTATION / FORMS

There are a few different forms that are used during a forensics investigation. These ensure that data is handled carefully and that actions are taken according to some predetermined plan. Here are examples of some forms that may be used during a digital forensics case:

**CHAIN OF CUSTODY:** This is a form that follows a certain piece of evidence, recording who has possession of that evidence and when. When a chain of custody form is used and someone tampers with evidence, the form can be consulted to see who was in possession of that evidence.

**INCIDENT RESPONSE PLAN:** An incident response plan is an organized approach to dealing with some type of incident. These may include who should be notified and what steps should be taken immediately after a certain incident is discovered.

**ESCALATION LIST:** This details who to notify and what actions to take when a security incident arises. The list ensures that the proper people are notified when a cyber incident is discovered.

# ESSENTIALS OF COMMUNICATION

Many things should be taken into consideration when deciding how to communicate regarding a cyber event, and who should be given what information. Though it may seem like communication is solely a human resources or marketing job, many of the responsibilities surrounding how a cyber event are communicated, both internally and to the public, can impact confidentiality, integrity, and availability of information.

With any communication surrounding a cyber event, it is important to first consider the legal repercussions of disclosing the event. It might be the case that sensitive information regarding the cyber incident would be illegal to disclose to the public. It could also be the case that certain legislation makes it imperative that disclosures happen in a certain way and/or during a certain timeframe. Whichever is the case, it's important to know legality issues must be considered when disclosing a cyber event.

Also, it is important to consider the future impact that disclosed information could have. It's a good idea, generally, to disclose what will be imperative, or helpful, and nothing more. Disclosing specific used protocols or network weaknesses after a cyber event could hurt security in the future. In order to ensure that communication about a cyber event happens in an orderly manner, and that various goals and considerations are achieved, an incident response plan is important.

An incident response plan is a formal plan outlining the steps that should be taken after a cyber incident occurs. These plans are concerned with how to limit the scope of impact and while responding to security events as they occur. They may also include specific instructions on how to best handle communication about a cyber incident.

When communicating about a cyber event, here are some goals to consider:

**REASSURANCE:** If the breach becomes public, it may be important to reassure stakeholders, customers, and the general public that steps are being taken to contain the damage and ensure that a similar breach does not occur later.

**BE PRECISE & HONEST:** It's important to communicate clearly and honestly. Aside from being wrong, being speculative or dishonest could hurt public trust in a company.

**CONSIDER THE LEGAL RAMIFICATIONS:** Lawsuits often occur as a result of cyber incidents. Companies should keep this in mind as they decide which information to make public.

## STAKEHOLDERS

Stakeholders are individuals with an interest in a company. These might be investors with a financial reason for wanting to know the status of a company. They could also be employees of a company. When communicating with stakeholders, consider the information from a few different vantage points. Considering the situation from an HR perspective, employees should be treated with dignity and respect while communicating a cyber event; the same is true for investors.

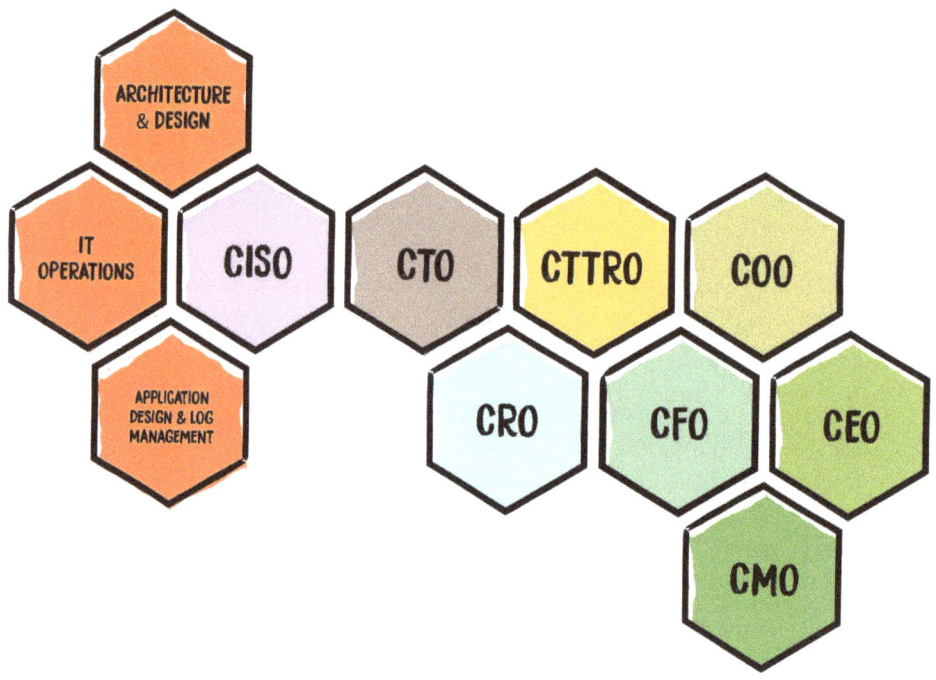

Another vantage point to think about when communicating with stakeholders is a legal one. A cyber event could occur within many different domains, resulting in more than one law that governs how all of this communication should occur. For example, financial institutions have different legal responsibilities than ice cream companies have regarding communicating about cyber events. It's important to follow and stay up to date with relevant legal requirements.

Also, communication about cyber events should be considered from a marketing perspective. It's important to communicate about the event in an honest way, but also one that makes the company look as good as possible. This could include sharing information about what steps are being taken to remediate the incident that occurred, as well as what will happen to ensure that a similar event doesn't happen in the future.

Finally, communication should be viewed from a management perspective. While cyber incidents vary, it is generally good to account for the impact that communication has on the employees and their ability to perform their jobs.

## PURPOSE OF COMMUNICATION PROCESSES

Communication about a cyber incident is a sensitive affair. This is why many incident response plans dictate how communications should occur, and who is entitled to what information. In general, keep the purpose of the communication in mind and do not communicate too much. There are a few good rules of thumb that can help companies to achieve this goal.

First, it is a good practice to limit sensitive information to trusted parties. Following a cyber incident, it is important to control the information being disclosed to the public, while ensuring that only trusted parties receive private information.

Secondly, it's important to prevent the inadvertent release of information. One smart way of doing this is to have protocols that dictate how communication about sensitive information should occur. This may include using encryption when discussing events online.

## ROLE-BASED RESPONSIBILITIES

When deciding on how to communicate about a cyber incident, consider the person's role. It's best to release information on a need-to-know basis. If someone is in a technical role responding to the cyber event, they may need specific information regarding what vulnerability was taken advantage of when the attack happened. It's important to give people information so that they can do their job, but not to share information when it is not needed. Remember every organization is going to be different with regard to roles and responsibilities.

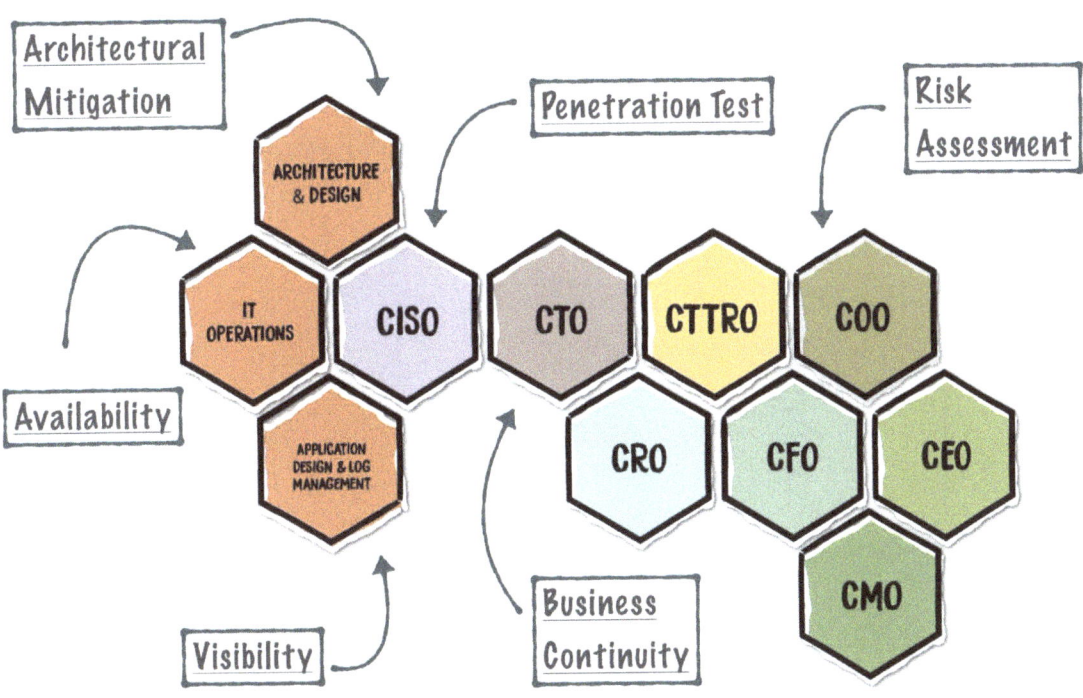

## RETAIN INCIDENT RESPONSE PROVIDER

Lastly, it may be a good idea to retain an incident response provider. An incident response provider is a company that has specific capabilities for handling cyber incidents. Organizations can choose to pay these providers fees regularly so that when a cyber incident ever does occur, they can have help with the response.

# INCIDENT SYMPTOMS & RECOVERY

## CONTAINMENT TECHNIQUES

Containment is one of the most important steps to take when recovering from an incident. We'll cover some preemptive steps that can ensure that the containment process is simple, as well as steps that can be taken to limit the impact of a security event after it has been discovered.

SEGMENTATION: One of the most important ways to contain and mitigate the impact of an attack. Network segmentation involves dividing the network such that one part can be accessed without compromising the rest. This example shows a firewall dividing the the intranet, DMZ, and internet.

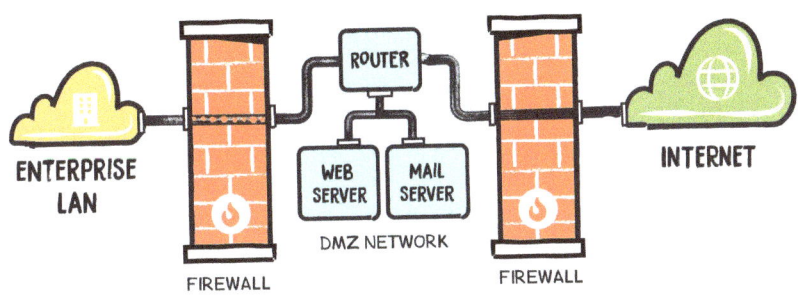

However, networks can be segmented even further. Consider this example, where inside of the intranet there are user workstations and a database with sensitive information:

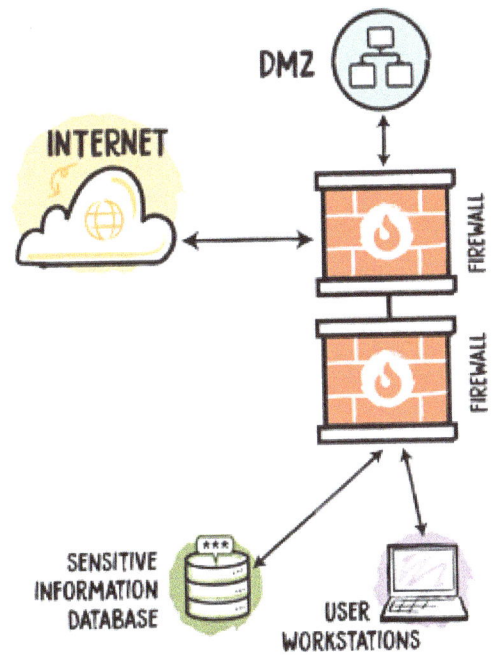

Dividing a network so that a breach in one part of the network doesn't necessarily mean that all parts are compromised is a good way to mitigate security threats.

Segmentation can be done before a cyber incident is ever detected. If a cyber event is detected, it might be wise to increase the segmentation to isolation.

**ISOLATION:** When an infected portion of a network is segmented such that it cannot affect other systems. The purpose of this is not to remove the attacker from the isolated system, but to limit the effect that an attacker can have on the rest of the network.

There are a few different ways to isolate a portion of the network. One way is to put this portion on its own, isolated VLAN so that the attacker cannot access other parts of the network. Or, a simple approach would be to isolate the network segment with firewall rules to limit the attacker's reach on other portions of the network.

**REMOVAL:** This falls under the umbrella of containment, though it is more intense than isolation or segmentation. With removal, affected systems are completely taken out of the network. This can be done by physically removing any connections from the infected system.

The implementations and purposes of segmentation, isolation, and removal might have some overlap. Just remember that these three are on a spectrum of containment aggression, with segmentation being the least severe, followed by isolation, and then the most severe, removal.

**REVERSE ENGINEERING:** The act of looking at a completed product to determine how it works.

In cybersecurity, many times professionals find that they need to reverse engineer malware to see what it does. Malware authors can be tricky and they don't leave notes in their code about how it works. Furthermore, malware authors might write their code in strange ways to obfuscate true behavior. So, cybersecurity professionals reverse engineer malware to learn its behavior, which is necessary to evaluating unknown software left on a network by an attacker during an incident.

## ERADICATION TECHNIQUES

After the cyber incident is contained to limit the amount of harm, it is time to eradicate any changes that were made during the security incident. The purpose of eradication is to dispose of all malware, secure the environment, and to get the affected parts of the network back to the same working order that they were in prior to the attack. It's also important to correctly dispose of anything that could lead to a subsequent attack or data leak.

If possible, it may be desirable to simply erase all of the data on a machine so that it can be used after the security incident. In extreme cases, however, it may be imperative to destroy unusable hardware to prevent further damage. The following types of sanitization, what they involve, and how they should be performed are from a chart developed by NIST (Source: NIST 800-88):

**DISPOSAL:** Disposal is the act of discarding media with no other sanitization considerations. This is most often done by paper recycling containing non-confidential information but may also include other media.

**CLEARING:** Clearing information is a level of media sanitization that would protect the confidentiality of information against a robust keyboard attack. Simple deletion of items would not suffice for clearing. Clearing must not allow information to be retrieved by data, disk, or file recovery utilities. It must be resistant to keystroke recovery attempts executed from standard input devices and from data scavenging tools. For example, overwriting is an acceptable method for clearing media. There are overwriting software or hardware products to overwrite storage space on the media with non-sensitive data. This process may include overwriting not only the logical storage location of a file (e.g., file allocation table) but also all addressable locations. The security goal of the overwriting process is to replace written data with random data. Overwriting cannot be used for media that are damaged or not writeable. Media type and size may also influence whether overwriting is a suitable sanitization method. [SP 800-36]. Studies have shown that most of today's media can be effectively cleared by one overwrite.

**PURGING:** Purging information is a media sanitization process that protects the confidentiality of information against a laboratory attack. For some media, clearing media would not suffice for purging. However, for ATA disk drives manufactured after 2001 (over 15 GB) the terms clearing and purging have converged.

A laboratory attack would involve a threat with the resources and knowledge to use nonstandard systems to conduct data recovery attempts on media outside the normal operating environment. This type of attack involves using signal processing equipment and specially trained personnel. Executing the firmware Secure Erase command (for ATA drives only) and degaussing are both examples of acceptable methods for purging. Degaussing a hard drive assembly usually destroys the drive as the firmware that manages the device is also destroyed. Degaussing exposes the magnetic media to a strong magnetic field in order to disrupt the recorded magnetic domains. A degausser is a device that generates a magnetic field to sanitize magnetic media. Degaussers are rated based on the type (i.e., low energy or high energy) of magnetic media they can purge. Degaussers operate using either a strong permanent magnet or an electromagnetic coil.

Degaussing can be an effective method for purging damaged media, for purging media with exceptionally large storage capacities, or for quickly purging diskettes.

Degaussing is not effective for purging non-magnetic media, such as optical media [compact discs (CD), digital versatile discs (DVD), etc). [SP 800-36, Guide to Selecting Information Security Products]

If purging media is not a reasonable sanitization method for organizations, this guide recommends that the media be destroyed.

**DESTROYING**: Destruction of media is the ultimate form of sanitization. After media is destroyed, they cannot be reused as originally intended. Physical destruction can be accomplished using a variety of methods, including disintegration, incineration, pulverizing, shredding, and melting.

If destruction is decided upon due to the high security categorization of the information or due to environmental factors, any residual medium should be able to withstand a laboratory attack.

### DISINTEGRATION, INCINERATION, PULVERIZATION, & MELTING
These sanitization methods are designed to completely destroy the media. They are typically carried out at an outsourced metal destruction or incineration facility with the specific capabilities to perform these activities effectively, securely, and safely.

### SHREDDING
Paper shredders can be used to destroy flexible media such as diskettes once the media is physically removed from its outer containers. The shred size of the refuse should be small enough that there is reasonable assurance in proportion to the data confidentiality level that the information cannot be reconstructed.

Optical mass storage media, including compact disks (CD, CD-RW, CD-R, CD-ROM), optical disks (DVD), and magneto-optic (MO) disks must be destroyed by pulverizing.

## VALIDATION

When all of the compromised systems have been adequately sanitized, it's time for validation. Validation is the act of ensuring that the recovery measures were successful and that a similar attack would be prevented.

One of the first and most important things to validate is that all of the machines on the system have been patched appropriately. Remember, patching is the process of installing updates from a manufacturer to eliminate known vulnerabilities. It is important to validate the permissions assigned to different accounts using the principle of least privilege to dictate which accounts need which privileges. After these and other changes are made, it is best to use a vulnerability scanner to scan all systems for vulnerabilities that need to be remediated.

Finally, it's important to make sure that all of the systems are logging correctly, and that these logs are being monitored by the appropriate systems, such as IDSs and IPSs.

## CORRECTIVE ACTIONS

After the impacts of an incident have been remediated, and affected systems are sanitized, validated, and back on line, security professionals reflect on what went wrong and right in the incident response process. It is important to have a formal 'lessons learned' session in which participants of the incident response process suggest changes that can be incorporated into the incident response plan.

## INCIDENT SUMMARY REPORT

The final step in remediating a security incident is to create an incident summary report. This report details the events that took place, the causes of those events, the impact of the incident, and all efforts that were taken to remediate the events.

This document serves several purposes. First, it helps to ensure that employees will remember and learn from such events. Secondly, it highlights ill-advised actions that were taken so that the incident response plan can be altered. Thirdly, this document might be used in subsequent legal battles to communicate what steps were taken in the incident response process.

# Relational Security Practices

# REGULATORY COMPLIANCE

Regulatory compliance was discussed earlier as a component of vulnerability management. Note that regulatory frameworks can fall under relational security practices. The regulations with which a company must comply depends on the industry. There is no catch-all rule for complying with the proper agencies. Compliance requires research and obtaining legal counsel from experts. As a refresher, this section will go through some of the most common regulations.

One example of regulatory compliance is HIPAA, or the Health Insurance Portability and Accountability Act. HIPAA regulates the handling of health data and articulates the technical controls that should be used in protecting information. The following excerpt from HPAA discusses access control:

> Regardless of the technology or information system used, access controls should be appropriate for the role and/or function of the workforce member. For example, even workforce members responsible for monitoring / administering information systems with EPHI, such as administrators or super users, must only have access to EPHI as appropriate for their role and/or job function.
>
> Four implementation specifications are associated with the Access Controls standard.
>
> 1. Unique User Identification (Required)
> 2. Emergency Access Procedure (Required)
> 3. Automatic Logoff (Addressable)
> 4. Encryption and Decryption (Addressable)

Source:
www.hhs.gov/sites/default/files/ocr/privacy/hipaa/administrative/securityrule/techsafeguards.pdf

GLBA, the Gramm-Leach-Bliley Act, is a regulatory act that dictates how financial institutions should handle data.

While HIPAA and GLBA address the handling of data, neither specifies how a specific vulnerability management program should be implemented.

For specifics on vulnerability management programs, you might reference FISMA (the Federal Information Security Management Act). FISMA applies to government agencies to ensure that specific controls are put into place depending on the criticality of maintaining confidentiality, integrity, and availability of a system.

The Payment Card Industry Data Security Standard, or PCI DSS, is actually a standard, not a law, maintained by the Payment Card Industry Security Standards Council. This includes details on how often organizations must run vulnerability scans, who can conduct those scans, and how discovered vulnerabilities should be resolved. It also includes standards on which encryption protocols and key sizes to use. With PCI, AES with a 128 bit key size or higher, TDES/TDEA, RSA with 2048 bits or higher, ECC with 224 bits or higher, and DSA/D-H with 2048/224 bits or higher are all acceptable methods of encryption.

As was stated earlier, the regulations with which a company must comply are determined by the business type. Ensuring that a company is doing everything possible to achieve and maintain a state of compliance involves researching industry-specific regulations and seeking legal counsel.

# FRAMEWORKS & CONTROLS

**FRAMEWORKS:** For a security professional in charge of ensuring confidentiality, integrity, and availability for a company, it may be difficult to ensure the creation of proper security procedures for every aspect of the business. There are so many controls and policies that must be created in any organization that the task of recording these and ensuring that they are all up to date with the most secure standards can seem nearly impossible. Adopting a security framework allows the deployment of policies and practices without creating them from scratch.

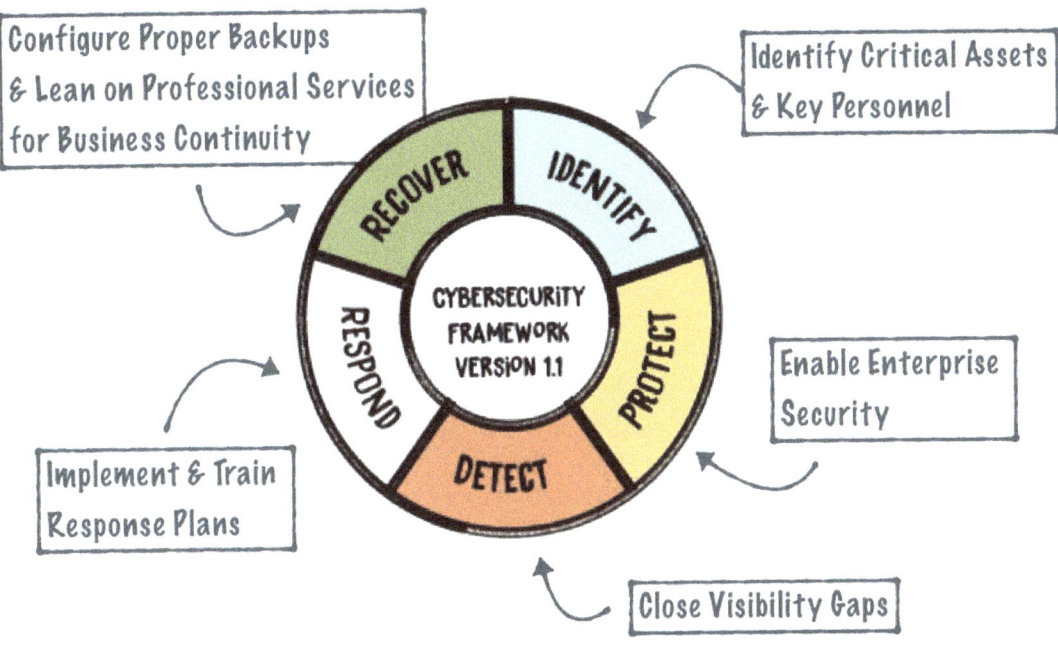

The following standard security frameworks are available to give companies guidelines and policies for many of their required security tasks.

**NIST:** The National Institute for Standards & Technology. NIST framework is one of the most popularly adopted frameworks for developing standards for both the U.S. federal government and companies in the private sector. According to NIST, the goal of the framework is to enable organizations to:
1. Describe their current cybersecurity posture
2. Describe their target state for cybersecurity
3. Identify and prioritize opportunities for improvement within the context of a continuous and repeatable process
4. Assess progress toward the target state
5. Communicate among internal / external stakeholders about cybersecurity risk

Source:
https://nvlpubs.nist.gov/nistpubs/CSWP/NIST.CSWP.04162018.pdf

The NIST framework is flexible. Depending on a company's security posture and goals, the standards that they are asked to adhere to change.

**ISO 27001:** The International Organization for Standards publishes the ISO 27001 framework. It's similar to NIST framework in that it sets guidelines that companies can choose to comply with if they desire a higher degree of information security. A company can undergo an assessment to become certified ISO 27001 compliant.

**COBIT:** Stands for Control Objectives for Information & Related Technologies. It is made by the Information Systems Audit and Control Association (ISACA).

**SABSA:** Sherwood Applied Business Security Architecture. The framework approaches security from different 'views.' For example, a 'Builder's View' includes thinking about physical security with respect to the architecture of a building.

**TOGAF:** Stands for The Open Group Architecture Framework. This is a common approach used in enterprise architecture. This framework defines things such as the interaction between business processes.

**ITIL:** Information Technology Infrastructure Library is another framework that offers a different information security strategy which companies might choose to follow.

**CONTROLS:** Once an organization adopts a framework and establishes certain security goals and objectives, they may want to implement controls. These may be based on specific criteria from their framework, and may differ from organization to organization depending on organizationally defined parameters such as budget.

**PHYSICAL CONTROLS:** These are physical things that can help to secure an environment. These might include fences, mantraps, fire alarms and security guards.

**LOGICAL CONTROLS:** These are technical controls that use logical rules to help meet a security standard. Examples of these might include firewall rules, role-based privileges, or password rules.

**ADMINISTRATIVE CONTROLS:** These are procedural practices that can help maintain a certain level of security. Examples might include procedures for vetting potential new hires, log review processes, and separation of duties policies.

## POLICIES & PROCEDURES

In order to increase confidentiality, integrity, and availability, organizations will create and adopt policies and procedures. Policies are statements of intent that guide an organization's actions. Procedures are decrees that specific actions must be followed. The following section reviews some common policies and procedures relating to information security.

**POLICIES:** As stated earlier, policies describe the importance of specific ideas and intentions for a company, or the goals that they would like to achieve. They do not prescribe the specific actions that an organization should take to achieve these goals. The following are examples of policies:

**PASSWORD POLICY:** States an ideal for password requirements. These might include requirements for password expiration intervals, limit the number of password resets, limit how often users can recycle former passwords, set password length and whether special characters should be permitted or required, and other constraints.

**ACCEPTABLE USE POLICY:** Dictates how a system or service should be used. This may include actions that are not permissible on that system, such as downloading malware onto a company computer, or other general guidelines that users might be required to accept prior to using a system.

**DATA OWNERSHIP POLICY:** This states explicitly who owns certain data. For example, a company may allow a user to use a free service, but the company would then collect and own data from that session.

**DATA RETENTION POLICY:** This policy outlines how long specific data will be retained. An example of this would be the amount of time that a police force holds onto evidence regarding a cold case before that evidence is destroyed.

**ACCOUNT MANAGEMENT POLICY:** This addresses account management, including requirements that must be met before a user can obtain an account, what authority / access different accounts allow users, and how / when accounts are deleted.

**DATA CLASSIFICATION POLICY:** This policy dictates how data should be labeled and classified. Institutions that label information 'classified' or 'protected' may have a policy dictating the data qualities required for such classifications.

**PROCEDURES:** These dictate specific actions and the circumstances that initiate those actions. For instance, a procedure might describe actions triggered by certain events, or periodic actions occurring at regular intervals to ensure policy goals are met.

> **CONTINUOUS MONITORING:** Procedures for continuous monitoring can dictate how the organization should be monitored and audited. This could refer to continuous monitoring by a vulnerability scanner, but it is also broader than that. It could also refer to scheduled monitoring of employees' clock-in/clock-out times, or any other events that may benefit from continuous, scheduled monitoring.
>
> **PATCHING:** Patching procedures dictate steps for identifying the need for a patch, as well as steps required prior to a patch being downloaded and installed. For example, the procedure might include instructions to install patches in a sandbox environment before implementation on a live machine in the organization's environment.
>
> **COMPENSATING CONTROL DEVELOPMENT:** The threat management section covered how compensating controls can be useful if a vulnerability cannot be removed from an environment. A compensating control development procedure includes instructions for determining which compensating controls are necessary, as well as how these controls should be tested and implemented.
>
> **CONTROL TESTING PROCEDURES:** These procedures test whether security controls are accomplishing the desired results without any adverse effects. For example, a fire alarm test would test whether that physical control was working.
>
> **MANAGE EXCEPTIONS:** Managing exceptions refer to how unanticipated or unexpected events should be managed. These might cover instances which require breaking from an established procedure. These exceptions also occur when an event is not addressed by any current procedure. Procedures made to manage exceptions identify who to consult when an anomaly occurs, and what authorization is required to break another procedure when confronted with an exception.
>
> **REMEDIATION PLANS:** These are steps that should be taken while remediating a cyber incident, and were discussed previously in the sections that dealt with incident response.

# VERIFICATION & QUALITY CONTROL

**AUDITS:** One way to ensure that an organization's security policies and procedures are adequate is to have them audited. An audit an examination or scrutiny of something. While more commonly used in reference to scrutinizing financial documentation, auditing security procedures / policies is a best practice among cybersecurity professionals.

There are two main types of audits, internal and external. An external audit is done by someone outside of the company. This could be a third party that is hired specifically for that audit. An internal audit is done by someone within the company. Both of these have their advantages. internal audits may be less expensive, while external audits could potentially be less biased. Regulations applied to particular industries may mandate regular external audits which must be conducted by unbiased third parties.

**EVALUATION & ASSESSMENTS:** These are tools that organizations can use to determine what risks they face, or how well their current security practices are being maintained.

An example of an evaluation is the Federal Finance Institution Examination Councils' cybersecurity assessment tool. Using this tool, an organization can determine its inherent risk to cybersecurity incidents and other important indicators. Another example of evaluation is a pen-test in which someone is hired by an organization to attack its network to gain information just as an attacker would. These can bring to light weaknesses in security protocols, procedures, or implementation.

A variety of options exist for assessing an organization's security competence. Among the most important to remember is that organizations can use vulnerability scanners to do a quick scan for network vulnerabilities. Reference the Risk Mitigation section for more examples of assessments.

**MATURITY MODEL:** A maturity model describes how well an entity responds when faced with adverse effects.

A company that consistently becomes more secure as a result of learning from cyber incidents would show growth in a maturity model.

For instance, a young company might view cybersecurity as a "necessary evil", but in time could grow to consider cybersecurity an integral part of its culture and continuing success.

One popular model is the Capability Maturity Model (CMM). This is a system that ranks processes from level 1 to level 5, with level 5 being the most developed.

**CERTIFICATION:** As discussed, many security frameworks exist that any organization can adopt as a part of developing policies and procedures. Several of these frameworks provide certification pathways to affirm that a company complies with its standards.

## COMMUNITY CYBER SECURITY MATURITY MODEL

|  |  |
|---|---|
| **LEVEL 1** Initial | • Minimal cyber awareness<br>• Minimal cyber info sharing<br>• Minimal cyber assessments and policy & procedure evaluations<br>• Little inclusion of cyber into Continuity of Operations Plan (COOP) |
| **LEVEL 2** Advanced | • Leadership aware of cyber threats, issues and imperatives for cyber security and community cooperative cyber training<br>• Informal info sharing/communication in community; working groups established; ad hoc analysis, little fusion or metrics; professional orgs established or engaged<br>• Autonomous tabletop cyber exercises with assessments of info sharing, policies & procedures, and fusion; routine audit program; mentor externals on policies & procedures, auditing and training<br>• Include cyber in COOP; formal cyber incident response/recovery |
| **LEVEL 3** Self-Assessed | • Leaders promote org security awareness; formal community cooperative training<br>• Formal local info sharing/cyber analysis; initial cyber-physical fusion; informal external info sharing/cyber analysis and metrics gathering<br>• Autonomous tabletop cyber exercises with assessments of info sharing, policies & procedures, and fusion; routine audit program; mentor externals on policies & procedures, auditing and training<br>• Include cyber in COOP; formal cyber incident response/recovery |
| **LEVEL 4** Integrated | • Leaders and orgs promote awareness; citizens aware of cyber security issues<br>• Formal info sharing/analysis, internal and external to community; formal local fusion and metrics, initial external efforts<br>• Autonomous cyber exercises with assessments of formal info sharing/local fusion; exercises involve live play/metrics assessments<br>• Integrate cyber in COOP; mentor externals on COOP integration; formal blended incident response and recovery |
| **LEVEL 5** Vanguard | • Awareness a business imperative<br>• Fully integrated fusion/analysis center, combining all-source physical and cyber info; create and disseminate near real world picture<br>• Accomplish full-scale blended exercises and assess complete fusion capability; involve/mentor other communities/entities<br>• Continue to integrate cyber in COOP; mentor externals on COOP integration; formal blended incident response and recovery |

# Security of Identity & Access Management

# CONTEXT-BASED AUTHENTICATION

Context-based authentication adds a layer of security to any system by determining who should be authenticated, using information about the user or the user's system.

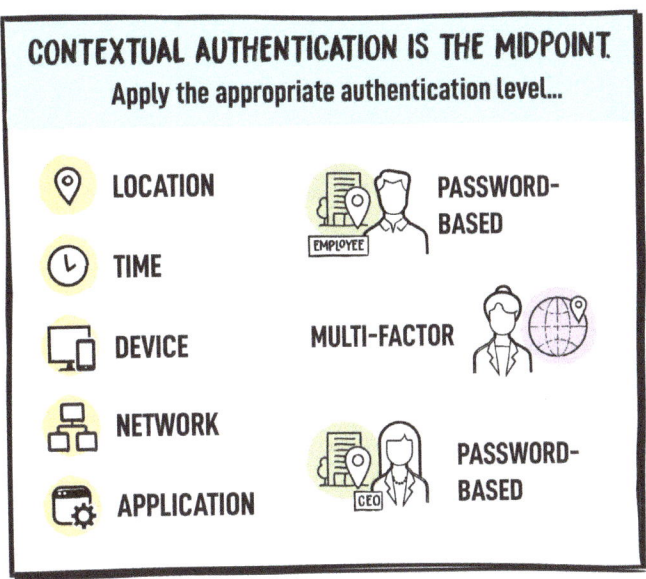

## TIME

Time of day is a common basis for authentication. For instance, a system might prohibit users from logging in outside of their typical work hours.

## LOCATION

Location is also a common context used in authentication. Location data can be collected from a user's GPS location or IP address. Credit card companies use location to authenticate purchases. If a card holder lives in Dallas, Texas and a transaction is attempted in Hong Kong, the credit card company may not authorize the transaction for fear that the credit card information was stolen.

## BEHAVIORAL

A user can also be authenticated based on behavioral patterns. For instance, we might expect a given user to access their account no more frequently than once per hour. If behavior-based authentication is in place, then an unexpected, increased frequency of access (in this case, multiple attempts within an hour) would induce the system to refuse to authorize the user.

Keystroke analysis relies on the unique patterns and timing of keystrokes made by a known user in order to authenticate that user. Such timing and patterns of keystrokes are generally unique to an individual. These patterns can be analyzed by machines to determine if someone is pretending to be someone else on a system.

# IDENTITIES & IDENTITY REPOSITORIES

## ISSUES ASSOCIATED WITH IDENTITIES

Accurately identifying unique individuals is central to sound security practices. If someone successfully poses as another individual, they could gain access to sensitive data or elevated privileges. An attacker can manipulate identity systems to gain unauthorized access in a variety of ways. This section will go through some common security issues associated with identities.

**PERSONNEL:** Identities are often associated with accounts in a system. Due to this, people often think only of technical attacks when considering security issues for identities. However, there are many identity-related attacks that are actually personnel-based.

Personnel-based attacks include threats such as insider attacks, in which an employee intentionally initiates an attack. Other examples include phishing and social engineering.

The best way to stop these kinds of identity security issues is to properly train all personnel. Employees are a possible point of failure if they handle their data incorrectly or are able to be tricked by a phishing email. Proper training can decrease the probability of an employee inadvertently doing something to grant an attacker unauthorized access to a system.

**ENDPOINTS:** These can also be vulnerable to identity attacks. These can include phones, tablets, and desktop computers. These attacks usually take place in the form of capturing credentials.

Examples of these would be screen capture applications, or keyboard capture applications or hardware. Other examples would include taking passwords, usernames, or tokens from local storage. All of these would be identity security issues relating to an endpoint.

**ROLES:** A role-based identity security issue is any attack that attempts to change a user's group or role so that they can have escalated rights and permissions.

**SERVERS & SERVICES:** Server-based identity security attacks can happen on servers that run identity services. These include any computer that runs an identity service on a network. The following section will go into more depth regarding some of these services and the security issues associated with them.

## ISSUES ASSOCIATED WITH IDENTITY REPOSITORIES

Next we'll go through some issues related to specific types of identity repositories.

**DIRECTORY SERVICES:** These provide information to network users about other users, network services, applications, and other data. One of the most popular directory services is LDAP, which stands for Lightweight Directory Access Protocol. With LDAP, the information gets stored in a hierarchical tree structure. There are many common directory services are built on top of LDAP, including ApacheDS, OpenLDAP, and Microsoft's Active Directory.

There are some potential security issues common to all of these implementations, because they are built upon LDAP. Many of these are taken care of with basic implementations of some services built on top of LDAP, but it's important to know about baseline LDAP deficiencies. These are some potential security guidelines that should be used with LDAP:

**ENCRYPTION PROTOCOLS:** Protocols such as TLS should be enabled. These will keep LDAP authentication secure.

**STORED PASSWORDS:** These should be encrypted. LDAP as an underlying service stores passwords as plaintext, so methods should be used to store passwords securely.

**SERVERS:** These should be replicated to provide redundancy. This way, if one server goes down, there is not necessarily a decrease in availability.

**ACCESS CONTROL LISTS:** These should be used to limit who has what permissions or access to data or services.

**ACCESS CONTROL RULES:** These should be put into place to decide who can modify what objects or rules. Because LDAP is widely used, there are a few attacks that are commonly seen with LDAP servers. These include:

*LDAP Injection Attacks:* These attacks use web applications that send queries containing input from a user. Attackers can inject LDAP queries or commands into these input boxes. These commands would come from the web application, and so the attacker would benefit from all of the rights and privileges that the web application had to send commands to the LDAP server. This can lead to unauthorized changes.

*Man-In-The Middle (MITM) Attacks:* These can try to exploit insecure connection protocol usage by capturing unencrypted traffic to gain information.

*Denial Of Service (DoS) Attacks:* In these attacks, a server is intentionally flooded with requests at such a rate that the server fails.

As stated earlier, many protocols are built using LDAP. Microsoft's Active Directory is one of the most common. In addition to all of the potential vulnerabilities and attacks that an LDAP server might face, be aware that the Active Directory could also have inherent vulnerabilities. It is important to use some form of patch management to ensure that all Active Directory specific vulnerabilities are patched as soon as possible. The same principle holds true for any service that runs on top of LDAP.

**TACACS+:** This protocol designed by Cisco is built upon TACACS to provide authentication, authorization, and accounting. TACACS+ is a service that handles authentication.

One vulnerability inherent in TACACS+ is that it does not check the integrity of data. This means that an attacker with access to the traffic could perform a replay attack. A replay attack is when data is intercepted by an attacker and then resent. So, an attacker could intercept data in transit that is being used to sign onto a service. This could then be resent by the attacker, giving him or her unauthorized access to some data, permissions, or services.

| RADIUS | TACACS+ |
| --- | --- |
| UDP 1812, 1645 (Authentication), 1813, 1646 (Accounting | TCP 49 |
| Created by IETF, Open Standard | Created by Cisco, Open Standard |
| Password Only | Full Packet Encryption |
| Unidirectional CHAP | Bidirectional CHAP |
| Low resource dependent | Requires more resources |
| No command logging | Full logging of commands |
| Used for network access | Supports administration |
| Authentication and Authorization is combined. Accounting is separate | Authentication, Authorization and accounting are separate. |
| Extensive accounting | Limited Accounting |
| Priviledge mode is supported | 15 priviledge modes are supported |

**RADIUS:** RADIUS is another AAA (authentication, authorization and accounting) network protocol. RADIUS stands for Remote Authentication Dial-in User Service and is one of the most common authentication systems.

One problem inherent in RADIUS services is that they use passwords that are obfuscated using an MD5 hash. This hash is now considered to be breakable, introducing a security issue associated with RADIUS services.

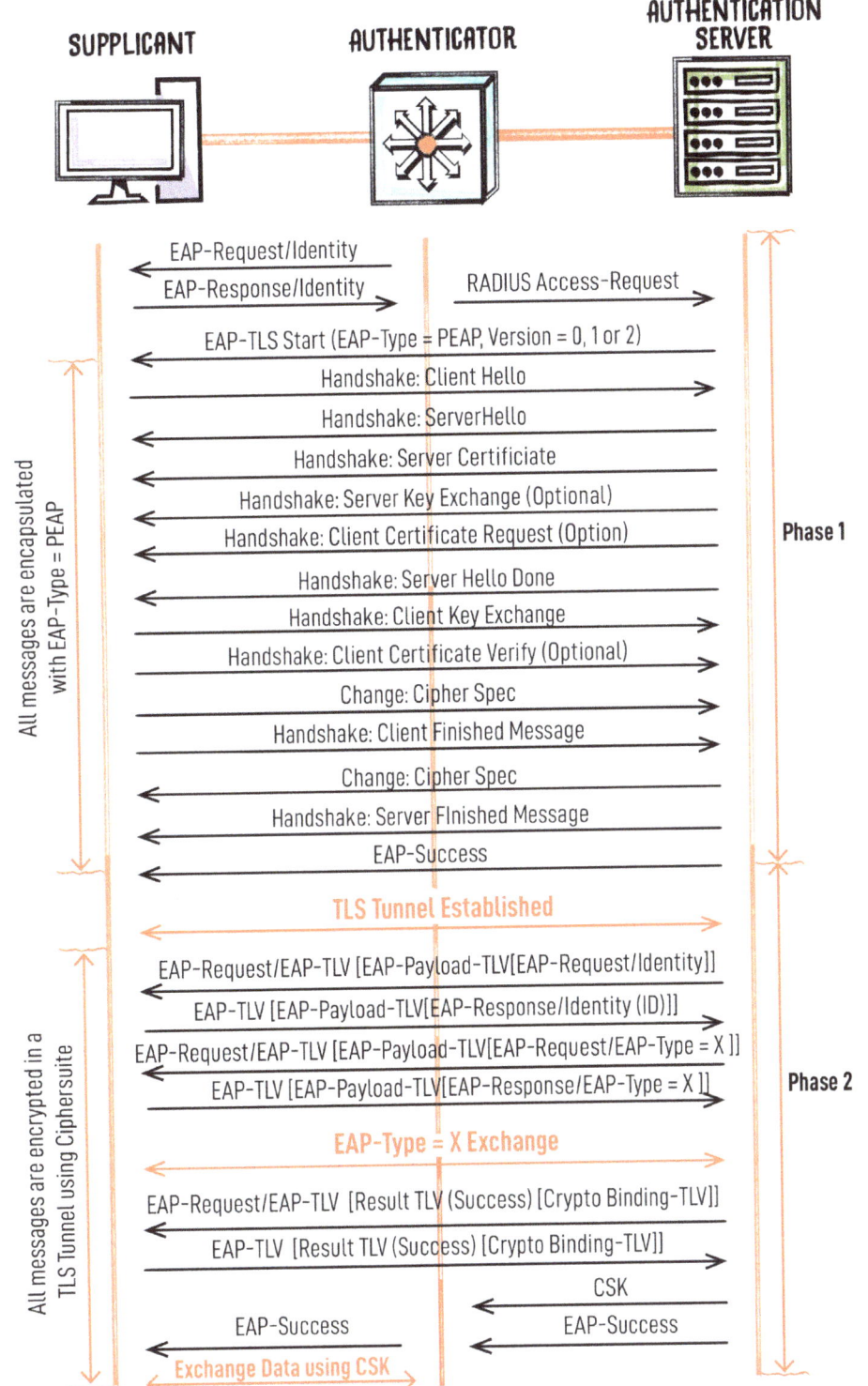

# FEDERATION AUTHENTICATION & SINGLE SIGN-ON

Single sign-on is an authentication system that allows users to authenticate once and gain access to multiple systems or services with only the use of one username and password.

Federated authentication refers to an outside source handling credentials and validating users. An example of this would be using a third party, such as Microsoft, to validate users to a network, rather than having the users login on a local server.

Single sign-on and federation authentication are often used together. For example, a company like Microsoft may handle authentication, and may also only require that users sign in once with one set of credentials to access multiple services. Such options are attractive for organizations because they outsource some of the security responsibility to other companies.

## SECURITY ISSUES

One obvious potential problem with federation and single sign-on is that it reduces the points of failure. So, if user credentials are uncovered by an attacker, he or she would then be able to access more systems than if the user had multiple different sets of credentials.

Something else to keep in mind when considering these schemes is manual versus automatic provisioning and deprovisioning. This is concerned with whether accounts can be created and deleted with or without manual oversight. Having manual oversight for the creation and deletion of accounts is more secure, but comes with the overhead of more work for administrators. This also means that there may be more delays for a user wanting to create an account.

Another thing to consider is whether or not to allow for self-service password reset. This could potentially be a security issue because it might allow an attacker with appropriate information about a user to reset the password and thus gain access.

# EXPLOITS

There are a lot of different exploits related to identity and access management. This section will go through some of the most common.

## IMPERSONATION

Impersonation is common to most exploits surrounding identity and access management. This isn't a specific attack, but rather the idea that an attacker is pretending to be someone else when trying to gain access to a system. The most common way to do this is by using stolen credentials. These credentials could be stolen in a variety of ways, such as brute force attacks or phishing.

## MAN-IN-THE-MIDDLE

These attacks happen as a result of an attacker intercepting information flowing over a network.

With regards to identity exploits, man-in-the-middle attacks include intercepting credentials from a user on their way to a server. These also include replay attacks, which were discussed earlier in the section about directory services. With replay attacks, information is intercepted as it travels from a host to a server and is then resent by an attacker. This could give an attacker unauthorized access. The main way to stop these attacks is to validate data sent to the servers and use secure encryption techniques.

## SESSION HIJACKING

This happens when an attacker takes over a user's session with a server. This could be done by getting a session key or cookie and then using it to take over a session. Session hijacking can be stopped by encrypting data as it travels over the network so that information cannot be stolen.

## CROSS-SITE SCRIPTING

XSS (Cross-Site Scripting) attacks are when an attacker is able to inject, or embed, a script on a webpage that will later run on other computers that visit the website. For example, if a website is vulnerable to XSS, it might have a comments box that allows a user to write javascript into it that would reside on the webpage.

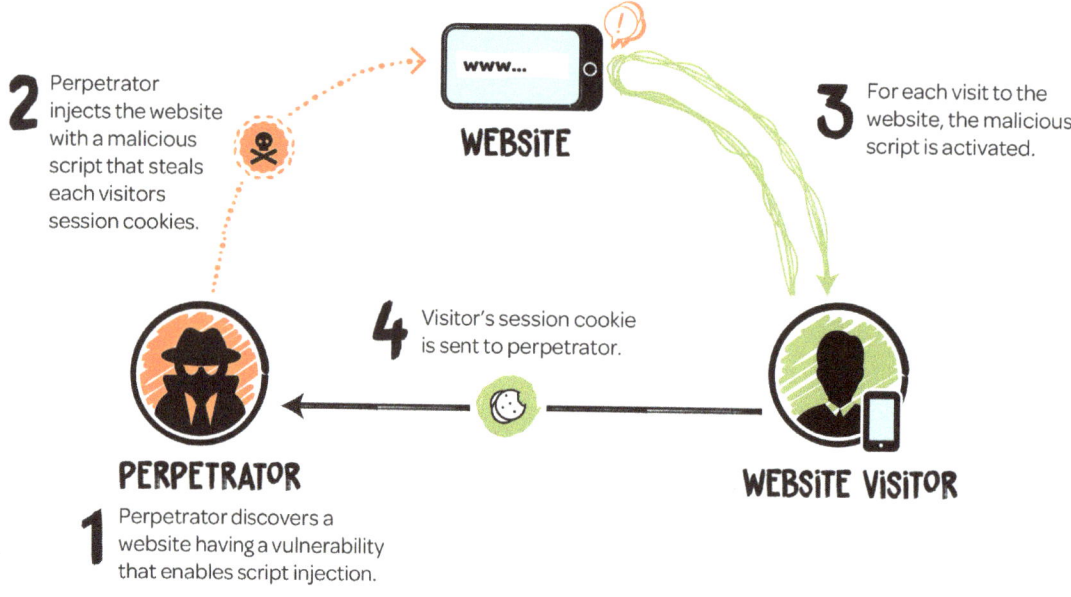

This could be used to capture credentials if the javascript was then embedded on a login page. The information input into the username and password boxes could then be sent to an attacker.

## PRIVILEGE ESCALATION

An attacker may gain initial system access through a user or service account with low privileges. A privilege escalation attack would then be used to elevate their permission level to admin or system level privileges. These attacks mostly focus on exploiting software or OS vulnerabilities. Patching all known vulnerabilities limits the probability of privilege escalation occurring

## ROOTKIT

A rootkit is a collection of tools that can help an attacker to gain access, escalate privileges, and hide in a network. A rootkit is not a single attack, but a collection of software that allows an attacker to carry out an attack and maintain a stealthy presence on a system.

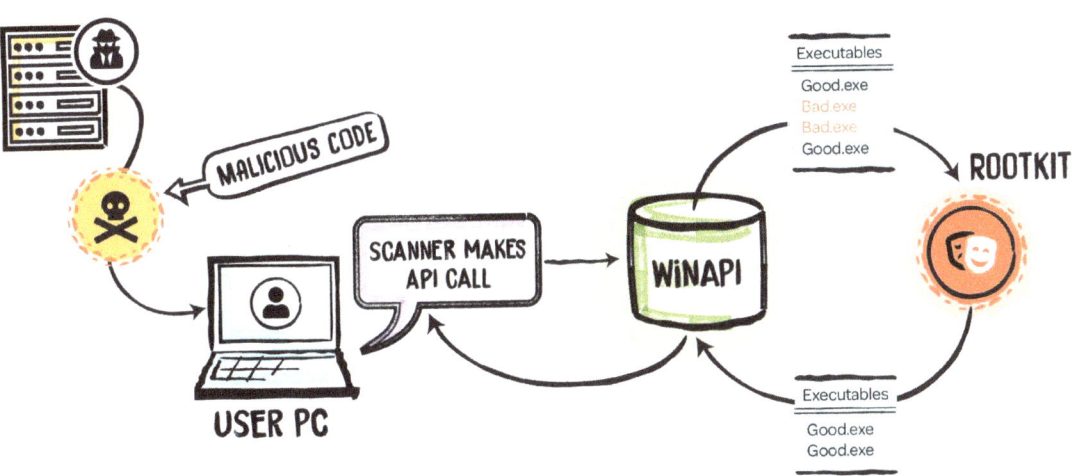

# Compensating Controls & Secure Coding

# SECURITY ANALYTICS & MANUAL REVIEW

## SECURITY DATA ANALYTICS

This involves monitoring and making sense of all of the different pieces of data that all of the different logs produce. Since a large amount of logs can be produced that comprise a great deal of data, manually reviewing all of these logs is not always feasible. To correct this, many organizations use automated analysis tools that look at logs and produce automated reports that are designed to help humans make sense of all of this information.

This is often achieved by using security appliances that perform data aggregation and correlation. Data is aggregated to a central location so that it can be analyzed by a security appliance. In this way, data from multiple different sources can be examined so that the analysis gives a fuller and clearer picture of what is going on in the network.

Let's review some types of analysis that are often applied to logs.

## TREND ANALYSIS

In simple terms, trend analysis looks at what has occurred in the past and uses this to make an educated prediction of what will occur in the future. This is helpful for spotting anomalies. If the network is trending towards having a certain amount of SSH traffic, and then data begins to vary widely from this trend, that would indicate a potential security event and something that would warrant further investigation.

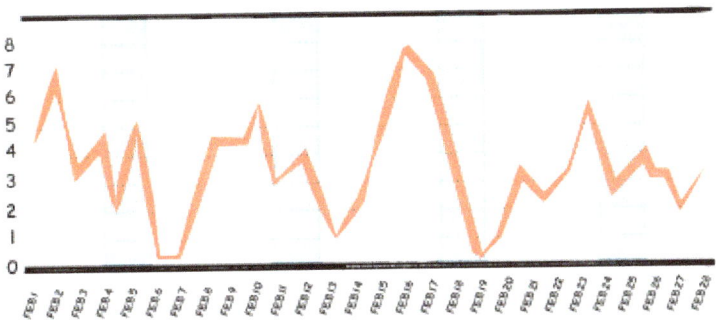

## HISTORICAL ANALYSIS

Historical analysis uses log information from the past to try to make sense of what might happen in the future. For example, if a company was involved in the online shopping industry, they may look at last year's Black Friday traffic and log records to get a better idea of what to expect the next Black Friday. This way, even if the traffic breaks from current trends, it is still expected and not flagged incorrectly as an anomaly.

## MANUAL REVIEW

Although it isn't feasible to manually review every log, there are certain logs that will require further investigation. These might be log events that devices using trend or historical analysis have found to be anomalies. Log monitoring systems may be set up to send notifications when logs outside the norm appear. If these logs are found to be part of normal traffic, they can be added to the baseline so that monitoring devices will not flag them in the future.

Any log may need to be reviewed manually, including firewall logs, authentication logs, syslogs, and event logs. For examples of different logs, see the reconnaissance results section.

Note that the manual review of logs can be a compensating control helps to ensure a more secure system. The reports generated by automated analysis are not always perfect. To correct this, it's a good idea to have humans review logs as a compensating control.

# DEFENSE IN DEPTH

Defense in depth is the concept of having multiple layers of security. In cybersecurity, this is one of the most used ideas to ensure availability, confidentiality, and integrity. This means that even if an attacker finds a clever way to circumvent some defensive strategy, there is still a safety net.

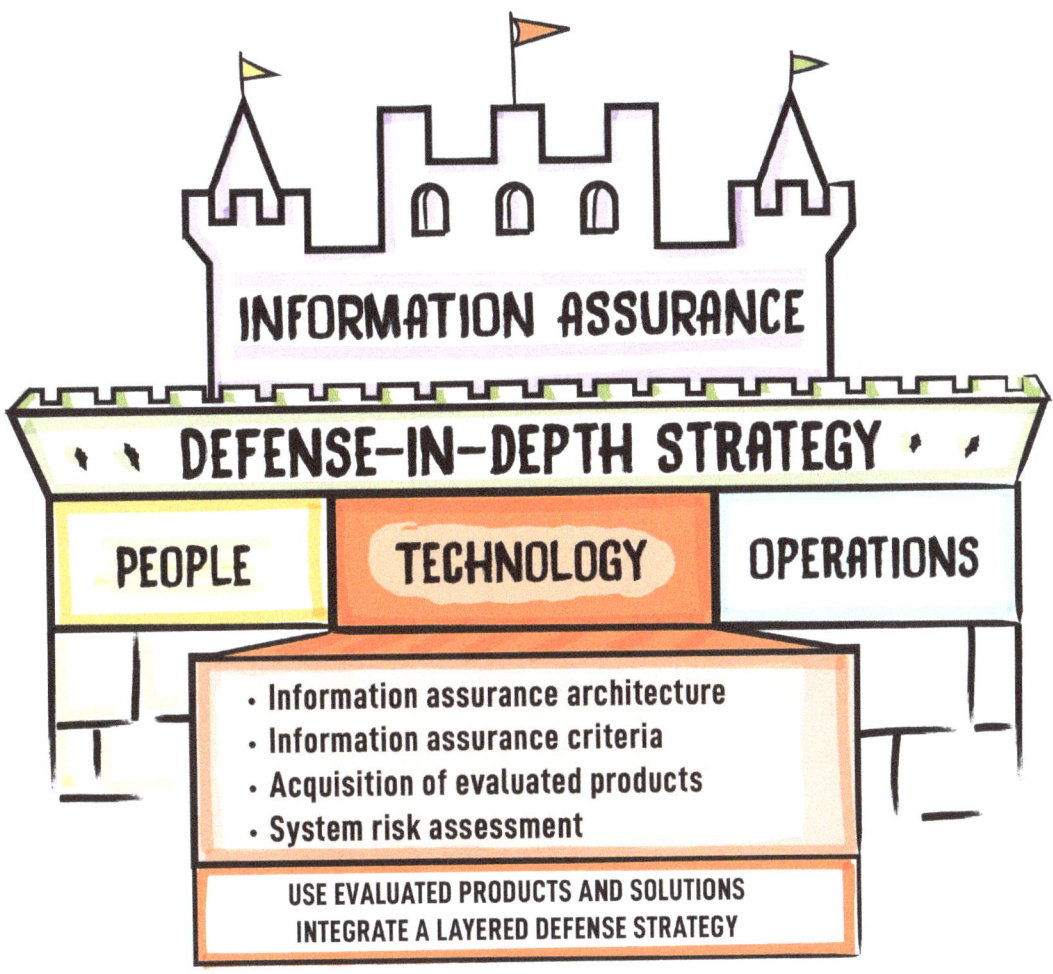

## PERSONNEL

An institution or organization is only as secure as its weakest link. It is a reality that organizations are not solely composed of devices and protocols. Human beings are intimately involved in nearly all business processes. Employees who are not well versed in cybersecurity or who are following insecure practices can be a vulnerability and target for attack in the same way that an unpatched server could be. Fortunately, there are things that can be done to ensure that the personnel and processes required to handle humans in a work environment are less vulnerable.

**TRAINING:** Proper employee training is a broad but important goal for an organization to strive for. Different companies may have different goals or needs when it comes to training, however, there are still things employees ought to understand.

It is important to train employees on any pieces of legislation the organization must comply with. This will go a long way towards mitigating the risk of a security incident due to an employee error, since many of these policies were designed with security as a goal.

An example of this is HIPAA compliance. When an employee goes through training to meet HIPAA compliance, he or she learns a lot about data privacy, what information is protected, and the steps to take to ensure that the environment remains secure.

Beyond the legislation that an organization should comply with, there are other things on which employees should be educated. These include how to select strong passwords, the importance of not downloading unauthorized software, understanding phishing and other social engineering tactics and how to avoid them, and the reasoning behind all of these practices.

Each organization will have unique needs which can be met with different training courses, but these training goals listed will provide a basic foundation to build from.

**DUAL CONTROL:** This is an administrative control that promotes higher security. When at least two employees are required to initiate a process, an organization is practicing dual control. This is important when a process can bring about a serious change in an organization, or hurt security if enacted under false pretenses. An instance when dual control is often implemented is when an organization has to write a check for a very large amount; a policy might state that two people of a certain status within the organization must sign checks over a certain value.

**SEPERATION OF DUTIES:** Another administrative control that can promote higher security. It is possible for employees to abuse their rights and privileges, hurting the security of an organization. To prevent this, separation of duties is often implemented. This is when more than one person is placed in control of a process that has the potential to be abused, such as, having several people approve time cards. If only one person approves time cards, they can ignore fraudulent numbers, giving advantages to themselves or their friends. With more than one person overseeing these, it becomes less likely that fraud will occur.

**THIRD PARTY/CONSULTANTS:** Even the most well-intentioned companies can overlook things in regards to administrative or technical controls that ensure strong security. As a compensating control, third parties are often brought in as consultants. They might offer a unique perspective and catch deficiencies in the security model.

**CROSS TRAINING:** This practice trains employees on tasks that coworkers typically perform. This has a few advantages. First, it offers protection if a critical coworker quits or cannot perform their job. Having only one person skilled in a critical domain allows a single failure point, so it is best to train others for the role. Secondly, cross training can ensure that new employees who may take on critical positions are properly vetted by others in the company. Thirdly, if no one in an organization knows about a particular domain, it is difficult to properly hire someone to perform that function.

**JOB ROTATION:** Beyond cross training, job rotation requires that employees totally move into a new position rather than just training for it. A job rotation structure provides similar benefits to cross training, enabling more of the workforce to understand critical functions. An added benefit of job rotation is that it prevents one person from controlling and abusing their position over a long period of time. This allows for the organization to find areas where fraud or misuses occur.

**MANDATORY VACATION:** This is when employees are forced to take some time off at regular intervals. The policy can make it easier to spot an employee who abuses rights and permissions to exploit the company without having to have long-term job rotation. This can be an effective administrative tool to ensure proper separation of duties; while a certain employee is not in the office, another employee is forced to take over that role for a time. If any exploitation has taken place, it is more likely to be found out during mandatory vacation.

**SUCCESSION PLANNING:** It is a reality that no one will work for a company forever, so planning a successor is a good idea. If an employee's abilities are so critical that the company would not survive without them, this is a single point of failure that needs to be remediated by training a successor to take over the role when the time comes.

## PROCESSES

Along with administrative controls for personnel, there are controls that should be in place for processes. The threat landscape may change over time, making some policies outdated while making new ones necessary to adopt.

One principal that's important when thinking about process change is continual improvement. It is important for organizations to always strive to strengthen their security, even in miniscule and incremental ways.

There are a few ways to achieve this goal. One is with scheduled reviews, which set aside time for an organization's security practices to undergo scrutiny. Under scrutiny, new policies and changes can be considered. Another way to meet this goal is with a proper retirement process, which lets go of old / outdated policies, redundant policies, or policies that are no longer deemed necessary.

## TECHNOLOGIES

Along with personnel and process control, there are some good, high-level technology practices indicative of strong security architecture. Many of these have been talked about in other sections before. Here is a brief overview of some of the things that may be seen in a security architecture:

**AUTOMATED REPORTING:** Security devices, such as vulnerability scanners or software for log analysis, can be set up to continuously monitor a network and generate reports that arrange the large amounts of data they analyze. This makes understanding what is going on in the network much easier for security professionals.

**SECURITY APPLIANCES:** A security appliance is a machine on a network that prevents unwanted traffic from reaching hosts on the network. There are a number of security appliances that should be on networks; these include firewalls and IDS/IPS.

**SECURITY SUITES:** These offer a variety of security products in one. Security suites may have anti-spam capabilities, built-in firewalls, and technology that detects malware.

**OUTSOURCING:** Companies are increasingly moving to cloud-based infrastructures, and as a result, outsourced security services (SECaaS) have become more popular.

**CRYPTOGRAPHY:** Cryptography is one of the most important ways to defend sensitive data. When reviewing security architectures, ensure that secure protocols are used so that traffic isn't going over the network in plain text. Also, passwords, usernames and other sensitive information should never be stored in plain text.

## OTHER SECURITY CONCEPTS (NETWORK DESIGN & SEGMENTATION)

Finally, when reviewing network architecture, it is important to look at the design. Network design can be crucial for security. Things to be considered are whether or not single points of failure exist on the network and whether or not the network is segmented properly.

Network segmentation limits the attack surface, meaning that the number of systems exposed to attackers is reduced. Segmentation also limits the impact of a security incident. If an attacker is able to gain access to one part of a properly segmented network, this doesn't necessarily mean that they will be able to gain access to the entire network.

# SOFTWARE DEVELOPMENT BEST PRACTICES

Rather than discussing security from the perspective of defending a network, this section reviews best security practices in relation to software development.

When a piece of software has been written, there are a few testing phases that should be used to ensure that the software is not vulnerable.

STATIC CODE ANALYSIS: Reviewing the text of a computer program for possible security issues. This can be done by another computer program that scans the program for vulnerabilities, or by another human that reads the code looking for security issues.

WEB APP VULNERABILITY SCANNING: Web application software can be scanned with a specific vulnerability scanner for web apps. These scanners review applications from the perspective of a black box to help determine if any vulnerabilities exist.

FUZZING: Fuzzing is the process of entering random or invalid data into a program to see how it handles unexpected data input. This can be helpful for spotting buffer overflow vulnerabilities.

## MANUAL PEER REVIEWS

Having peers manually review each other's code can be a great way to find vulnerabilities. There are a few common methods with which this can happen.

PASS-AROUND CODE REVIEW: In this method, developers send code to each other and all check each other's work for issues. This is a very informal method of peer review.

OVER-THE-SHOULDER REVIEW: Using this review method, one programmer writes code while another programmer watches for vulnerabilities as the code is written.

PAIR PROGRAMMING: Two developers work on the same piece of code at the same time, with one typing at the keyboard while the other watches. Here, the two developers converse while they are developing, discussing what to do and potential issues that could arise.

MANUAL PEER REVIEW: One of the most sophisticated methods is tool-assisted review of code. There are software-based tools that facilitate the process of code review, allowing programmers to quickly and effectively review code.

## USER ACCEPTANCE TESTING

User acceptance testing is a type of software testing in which the software is used under normal conditions by its intended users. This tests issues with functionality and security.

## STRESS TEST APPLICATION

Stress testing involves testing the application under a higher load than it is intended to handle. This may include using the program in such a way that it induces a race condition, or using it in such a way that it is abnormally demanding on the computer's resources.

## SECURITY REGRESSION TESTING

When vulnerabilities or bugs are discovered in a program, developers often release a patch to fix the specific problem. Patches can have unintended consequences, which is why security regression testing is necessary. Security regression testing checks all parts of an application after any part of the application has received a fix.

# SECURE CODING BEST PRACTICES

Just like best practices for network security, there are also best practices and frameworks used to ensure secure coding. There are many different frameworks that can be used to analyze coding practices and develop processes to ensure that secure approaches are practiced.

An example of an institution that gives secure coding practice guidelines is OWASP, which stands for the Open Web Application Security Project.

As an example, here is OWASP's checklist for general coding practices:

- Use tested and approved managed code rather than creating new unmanaged code for common tasks.
- Utilize task specific built-in APIs to conduct operating system tasks.
- Do not allow the application to issue commands directly to the Operating System, especially through the use of application initiated command shells.
- Use checksums or hashes to verify the integrity of interpreted code, libraries, executables, and configuration files.
- Utilize locking to prevent multiple simultaneous requests or use a synchronization mechanism to prevent race conditions.
- Protect shared variables and resources from inappropriate concurrent access.
- Explicitly initialize all your variables and other data stores, either during declaration or just before the first usage.
- In cases where the application must run with elevated privileges, raise privileges as late as possible, and drop them as soon as possible.
- Avoid calculation errors by understanding your programming language's underlying representation and how it interacts with numeric calculation. Pay close attention to byte size discrepancies, precision, signed/unsigned distinctions, truncation, conversion and casting between types, "not-a-number" calculations, and how your language handles numbers that are too large or too small for its underlying representation.
    - Do not pass user supplied data to any dynamic execution function.
    - Restrict users from generating new code or altering existing code.
    - Review all secondary applications, third party code and libraries to determine business necessity and validate safe functionality, as these can introduce new vulnerabilities.
- Implement safe updating. If the application will utilize automatic updates, then use cryptographic signatures for your code and ensure your download clients verify those signatures. Use encrypted channels to transfer the code from the host server.[1]

Other organizations like SANS and the Center for Internet Security also have guidelines for secure coding practices. These guidelines are extensive, offering security design recommendations and benchmarks that administrators can require developers to meet to increase a program's security.

---

[1] https://www.owasp.org/images/0/08/OWASP_SCP_Quick_Reference_Guide_v2.pdf

# TOOLS & TECHNOLOGIES

# PREVENTIVE & COLLECTIVE TOOLS

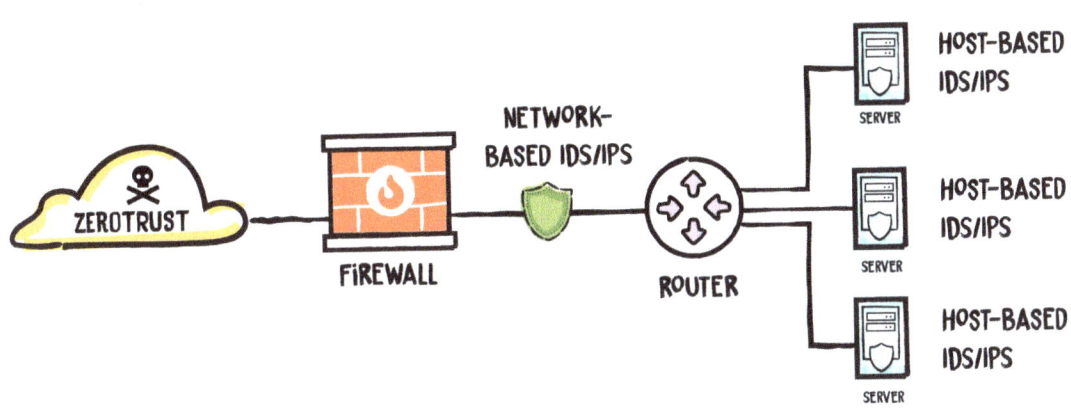

## IDS & IPS

Intrusion detection and prevention systems detect malicious traffic and engage prevention activities. Here are a few popular IDS and IPS engines that are available to consumers.

SNORT: Snort was the first IDS system, developed in 1998. It uses community developed rules to identify malicious traffic, and is now under Sourcefire, which is owned by Cisco.

SURICATA: Another IDS system is Suricata, developed by the Open Information Security Foundation (OISF), used to identify malicious traffic.

ZEEK (FORMERLY BRO): Zeek is an open source network monitoring tool. It performs signature analysis, anomaly detection, connection analysis, and application layer analysis to determine if traffic is anomalous or malicious.

## HIPS

A Host Intrusion Prevention System is, as the name implies, an intrusion prevention system that resides on a host. These detect malicious traffic from the point of view of a host, rather than sitting somewhere on a network and detecting traffic from an external point.

## FIREWALL

Firewalls play an important role in keeping a network secure. Firewalls look at traffic and decide whether or not to allow it to pass through a certain point on a network. These are important for keeping certain traffic out of networks, and also for network segmentation.

Palo Alto and CheckPoint are both companies that specialize specifically in firewalls. Also, traditional network device manufacturers such as Cisco and Juniper make firewalls as well.

## ANTIVIRUS & ANTI-MALWARE

Antivirus software is used to prevent, detect, and remove viruses. Anti-malware, another name for an antivirus, is used to detect, prevent, and remove many kinds of malware. Popular antivirus software vendors include Norton, McAfee, and Avast.

## DATA LOSS PREVENTION (DLP)

Many HIPS and antivirus vendors also create DLP software for host devices. Such software helps prevent the exfiltration of data from the business. Many times this comes in the form of blocking optical and flash media, but solutions exist that can monitor email traffic, too. When considering host-based software packages, DLP is an important consideration.

## EMET

The Enhanced Mitigation Experience Toolkit is a framework from Microsoft that provides an interface where users can configure security settings.

## WEB PROXY

A web proxy is a network device that sits on a network and serves as an intermediary between users and the internet. With a web proxy, a user makes a request to a proxy, which then sends a request to a web server. The web server responds to the proxy, which then sends information back to the user.

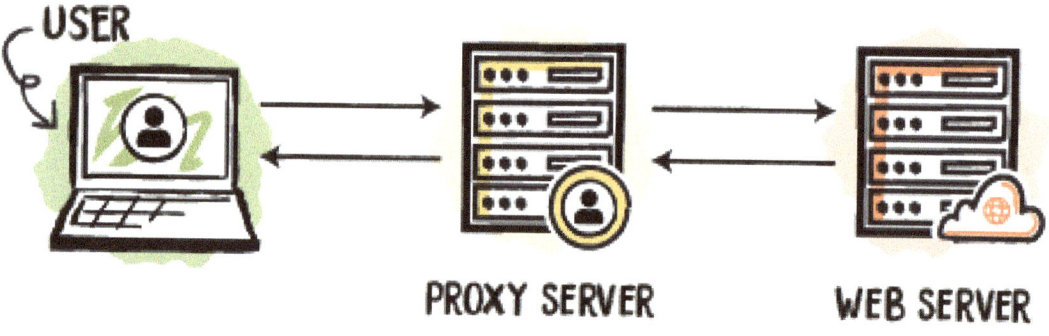

Web proxies serve two important functions. First, the proxy server can cache responses from web servers. This limits the amount of bandwidth a company may have going out to the internet and can save money in the long term.

Secondly, proxies are used to monitor and block traffic that violates a company's acceptable use policy. The proxy can act as a Man in the Middle, easily intercepting, modifying, and even decrypting web-based traffic.

## WEB APPLICATION FIREWALL (WAF)

Web application firewalls provide protection for web applications. These monitor and control access to certain services. WAFs have special capabilities to protect against many different common web application attacks, such as SQL injection. Some common WAF vendors include ModSecurity, NAXSI, and Imperva.

## SIEM

Security Information & Event Management (SIEM) systems can manage security and network information produced by various networking devices. Popular SIEM systems include ArcSight, QRadar, Splunk, AlienVault, OSSIM, and Kiwi Syslog.

**SPLUNK:** Splunk is a tool that is commonly used in situations where a large amount of data needs to be understood by the user. This tool is used in daily security operations monitoring as well as in incident response situations.

**ALIENVAULT:** Universal Security Manager is an AlienVault product that offers SIEM functionality.

**OSSIM:** This is an open source security tool that provides SIEM functionality.

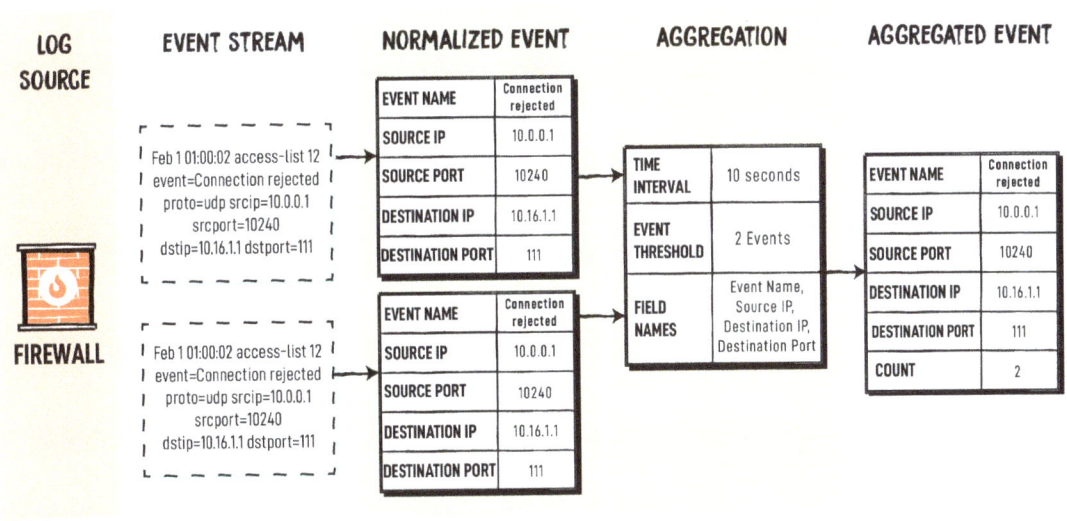

## HOW EVENT AGGREGATION WORKS

## NETWORK SCANNING

NMAP is an open source network discovery tool that is used for network discovery. With NMAP, it is possible to scan an IP address, or range of IP addresses, to see what responds to different types of probes and which ports are open on a target host. NMAP also interrogates services to identify the OS and version that a target machine is running.

## VULNERABILITY SCANNING

Vulnerability scanners examine specific hosts or a network to find known vulnerabilities. These are important for gathering information about a network as they reveal known vulnerabilities and suggest patches to download and install. There are several popular vendors for these:

**QUALYS:** Qualys produces QualysGuard, a network vulnerability scanner that can be utilized as a SaaS (software as a service) product. It can scan for vulnerabilities in the cloud and on premise.

**NESSUS:** Nessus vulnerability scanners are amongst the most popular options available.

Others include OpenVAS, Nexpose, Nikto, and Microsoft Baseline Security Analyzer.

## PACKET CAPTURE

Packet capture tools allow users to sort and examine specific packets that travel through certain points on a network.

**WIRESHARK:** The most popular packet capture tool. Wireshark allows users to filter the packets they are reviewing in a variety of ways, such as by IP address or protocol. Users can follow TCP, UDP, and HTTP streams, and much more, and Wireshark is available for free.

**TCPDUMP:** This is another free tool often used for packet capture. It is a command line tool that captures or displays packets and allows users to filter for specific packets using BPF expressions.

**NETWORK GENERAL:** The creator of the original packet analyzer tool released in the 1990's. This company is now under NetScout Systems.

**AIRCRACK-NG:** This packet capture and analysis tool is dedicated to wireless networks. The tool also allows users to test a wireless network to see if it is configured in a secure manner.

## COMMAND LINE / IP UTILITIES

Command line tools are popular among cybersecurity professionals because they are simple to use, lightweight, and are great for basic inquiries about a network or host.

**NETSTAT:** Netstat analyzes network information on a specific host and can display things such as active TCP and UDP connections. This can be used to see if a host is connected to something that it should not be.

**PING:** Ping is a tool that can allow users to see if a machine is active on a network. Ping sends out an ICMP message that a live machine, accepting ping requests, will respond to.

**TRACERT / TRACEROUTE:** Traceroute is a command line tool that sends out a signal to a domain and then lists all of the intermediate nodes between the computer that initiated the command and the one hosting the domain name.

**IPCONFIG / IFCONFIG:** Ifconfig is a quick way to get information about a network interface. This tool outputs information such as the network configurations and the subnet mask. Ipconfig is the equivalent command on a Windows OS.

**NSLOOKUP / DIG:** nslookup and dig are both tools that allow a user to input a domain name to get information about that domain name from a DNS system.

**SYSINTERNALS:** Sysinternals are a suite of tools available from Microsoft that allow users to examine things about a host. One example is Process Explorer, which allows users to see and learn about the processes currently running on their computers.

**OPENSSL:** OpenSSL is a suite of security applications that can secure the applications that are communicating over networks.

# ANALYTICAL TOOLS

## VULNERABILITY SCANNING

Vulnerability scanning can be an important analytical tool. Our two lessons on vulnerability scan output earlier give insight regarding the types of analytics gained by using vulnerability scanners. Of course, the most common analytics are those having to do with vulnerabilities. Such scanners can provide insight into the various aspects of vulnerabilities on a network, such as the number of vulnerabilities over time.

Here is an example of trends that can be output using a Nessus vulnerability scanner:

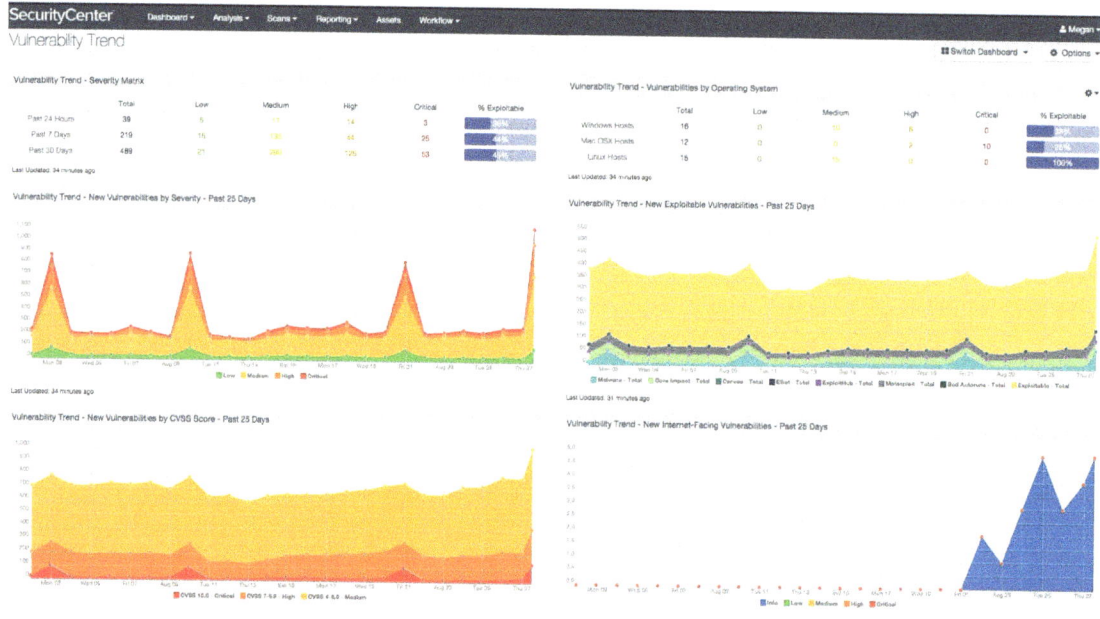

## SECURITY ANALYZER

Security analyzers are tools that allow users to monitor a network for outages, system resource usage, bandwidth usage, and other metrics. All of these allow users to better understand what is happening on their network and lead to better security. There are many common monitoring tools, such as MRTG, NAGIOS, SolarWinds, Cacti, and NetFlow Analyzer.

**MRTG:** Multi Router Traffic Grapher is a tool that uses SNMP to monitor network connections. This can be used to gather information about what is on the network as well as the topology.

**NAGIOS:** This monitoring tool allows users to download plugins that can provide analysis and reporting about events on a network.

**SOLARWINDS:** SolarWinds is a network monitoring tool vendor. Their tools allow users to see the state of various devices on a network, statistics on the protocols being used, and much more. In addition, users can get alerts and reports about events and the configurations in their networks.

**NETFLOW ANALYZER:** NetFlow analyzers are monitoring tools that help users understand information related to network flow, like bandwidth usage. They collect NetFlow traffic and aggregate it, allowing for user-friendly presentation and search functionality.

**CACTI:** This is a network monitoring tool that polls network devices (collecting SNMP data) and allows users to build graphs from the information.

## INTERCEPTION PROXY

Interception proxies are devices that are set up to catch traffic and then act as an intermediary. They receive information from the user, send the information to web servers, and then respond to the user. These can be used for malicious activities such as the unauthorized viewing of data or for injecting things into the traffic. For example, a person using one of these tools could send a user to a fake login page in a phishing attempt. Some tools allowing users to act as interception proxies are Burp Suite, Zap, and Vega.

# EXPLOITATION TOOL SETS

## FRAMEWORK

An exploit framework allows users to deploy different exploits on a system. This can be helpful in pen testing to check which exploits can be successfully run on a system.

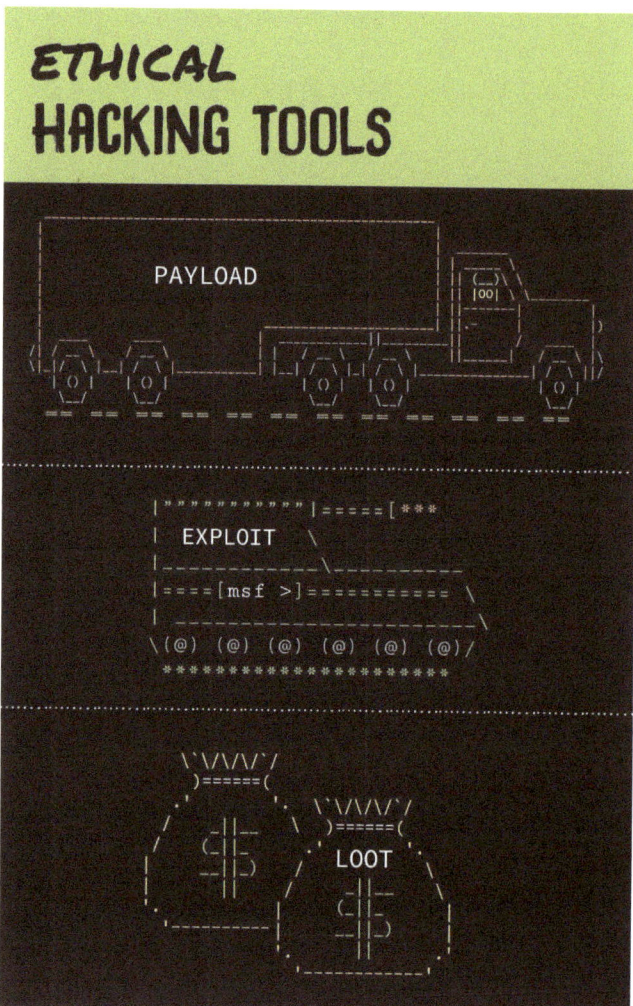

Metasploit is an open source exploit framework which contains over 900 different exploits. The framework allows users to choose an exploit and target, and then modify the payload to evade detection before deployment.

Metasploit attacks are frequently accompanied by vulnerability scans to test what is vulnerable on a system prior to attempting the exploit. One example is the Nexpose vulnerability scanner, which scans on Metasploit framework. This helps ensure that Metasploit payloads are successful.

## FUZZERS

Since tools such as vulnerability scanners can only check for known vulnerabilities, there are some limits. For example, attackers may discover that they can use a new, unknown exploit attack on an application.

One example of this is fuzz testing, in which unexpected input gets entered into a program in an attempt at finding a new exploit.

Fuzzers are applications that can automatically test a program using this method. Peach Fuzzer, Untidy, and Microsoft's SDL Regex are examples of available fuzzers that can serve an important role in software development, ensuring that abnormal input won't cause unexpected, negative effects.

# FORENSIC TOOLKITS

Forensic tools allow security analysts to investigate network events. They can help users get a better idea of what happened, and may be presented as evidence in court.

## FORENSIC SUITES

Forensic suites have multiple tools that can be used to conduct an investigation. These help with decryption, imaging, and other forensic tasks. Here are a few popular forensic suites:

**ENCASE:** EnCase is a forensic suite available from Guidance Software. It has several forensic functions and is often used to recover evidence on hard drives.

**FTK:** Forensic Toolkit (FTK) is a suite that allows usage of a variety of tools in a GUI environment.

**HELIX:** Helix is another suite of open source forensic tools that can help with investigations.

**SYSINTERNALS:** Sysinternals offers various tools for conducting investigations on Windows OSs.

**CELLEBRITE:** Cellebrite's suite includes dedicated tools for mobile device forensics.

## HASHING

In forensics investigations, it may be necessary to create a digital fingerprint of a file or drive. Hashing is a great way to do this. Two hashing algorithms that are popularly used in forensic analysis are MD5 and SHA. These tools can create a unique hash for a file, ensuring that it isn't altered in the investigation process. At the end, a file can be hashed again, and if it hasn't been altered, the algorithm will create the same hash value.

## PASSWORD CRACKING

Security professionals may enter a system using password cracking to acquire a password.

**JOHN THE RIPPER:** An open source utility that can be used to crack passwords on various OSs. It allows users to input word lists and password requirements to expedite the cracking process.

**CAIN & ABEL:** A password cracking tool able to perform network sniffing and VoIP decoding. It can also use more traditional means, such as brute force password cracking.

## IMAGING

In a forensics investigation, it may be important to create an exact copy of an image. DD, Disk Duplicator, is a popular utility that allows for this. DD is built into Linux and allows users to create an identical image copied from the original. Copies are frequently used by analysts to examine evidence without the risk of compromising the original data's integrity.

# NOTES

# GLOSSARY

| | |
|---|---|
| ACCEPTABLE USE POLICY | This is a policy that dictates how a system or service should be used. This may include actions that would not be permissible on that system (such as downloading malware onto a company computer) and other general guidelines that users may be required to accept prior to using a system. |
| ACCESS CONTROL LISTS | A list of rules that a router or firewall follows to determine which traffic should be allowed to pass through that node. |
| ACCOUNTING DATA | This is data used to account for the financial status of an entity. |
| ADMINISTRATIVE CONTROLS | These are procedural practices that can help to maintain a certain level of security. Examples might include procedures for vetting potential new hires, log review processes, and separation of duties policies. |
| ADVANCED PERSISTENT THREAT | An advanced persistent threat is a threat that infiltrates a network and persists for a long period of time, using advanced techniques. |
| ANOMALY ANALYSIS | Anomaly analysis looks at data points compared to a baseline to identify anomalies. |
| BUFFER OVERFLOW | When more input than expected is written into an input box, resulting in changes in memory beyond where the input box was supposed to be written to. |
| CHAIN OF CUSTODY FORM | This is a form that follows a certain piece of evidence, recording who has had possession of that evidence when. With a chain of custody form, if someone tampers with evidence, this form can be consulted to see who was in possession of that evidence. |
| DATA CLASSIFICATION POLICY | This is a policy that dictates how data should be labeled and classified. For example, institutions that label information as 'classified' or 'protected' may have a policy that dictates the qualities data may have to receive certain classifications. |
| DATA EXFILTRATION | Data exfiltration is when an attacker will try to get data out of a system or network. |
| DATA OWNERSHIP POLICY | This is a policy that states who owns certain data. For example, a company may allow a user to use a free service, but that company would then collect and own data from that session. |
| DATA RETENTION POLICY | This is a policy that outlines how long specific data will be retained. An example of this would be the amount of time that a police force holds onto evidence regarding a cold case before that evidence is destroyed. |

| | |
|---|---|
| DENIAL OF SERVICE ATTACK | DoS attacks are attacks in which a server is intentionally flooded with requests at such a rate that the server fails. |
| EXPLOIT FRAMEWORK | An exploit framework is a framework that allows users to deploy different exploits on a system. |
| FUZZ TESTING | Fuzz testing is when unexpected input is entered into a program in an attempt to find a vulnerability that might be exploitable. |
| HEURISTIC ANALYSIS | Heuristic analysis is when a system is analyzed for its behavior, or what it does. |
| INCIDENT RESPONSE PLAN | An incident response plan is an organized approach to dealing with some type of incident. These may include who should be notified and what steps should be taken immediately after a certain incident is discovered. |
| INDUSTRIAL CONTROL DEVICES | Industrial control devices are devices that monitor and control industrial applications. |
| INTELLECTUAL PROPERTY | This is creative property, such as a screenplay, that has some value and is owned by some entity. |
| INTRUSION DETECTION SYSTEM (IDS) | Intrusion detection systems (IDSs) are systems that are placed somewhere in a network and that monitor all traffic for suspicious activity. They typically monitor will look for things such as suspicious patterns or another type of behavior analysis method to determine if an administrator should be alerted to the traffic. |
| LOG | A log is a record of what has happened to a particular node on a network. |
| LOGICAL CONTROLS | These are technical controls that use logical rules to help meet a security standard. Examples of these might include firewall rules, role-based privileges, or password rules. |
| MAN-IN-THE-MIDDLE ATTACK | Man-in-the-middle attacks are concerned with attacks that happen as a result of an attacker intercepting information flowing over a network. |
| NETWORK ACCESS CONTROL (NAC) | Network access control (NAC) is a solution that helps organizations or any other user decides who is allowed to connect and who isn't allowed to connect to a network. |
| NETFLOW ANALYZER | Netflow analyzers are tools that can display and summarize network traffic and network usage. |
| NETWORK MAPPING | Network mapping is the act of discovering and representing the physical connections in a network. |

|  |  |
|---|---|
| NMAP | NMAP is an open source network discovery tool that is used to map a network. |
| PACKET ANALYZER | A packet analyzer is a piece of software that can give a user information about individual packets. These can also be referred to as packet sniffers. |
| PASSWORD POLICY | A password policy lists the ideal for password requirements. These may include requirements for a minimal amount of time that a password should exist, a maximum amount of time that a user can have a password, how often users can recycle passwords, password length, if special characters should be permitted or required in a password and other things like this. |
| PATCHING | A patch is a piece of software that can take care of vulnerabilities or functional issues. |
| PAYMENT CARD INFORMATION | This is information relating to a payment card that could be used to make unauthorized purchases in someone else's name. |
| PERSONAL HEALTH INFORMATION | This is health information that the government has deemed to be protected, such as diagnosis or medical treatments. |
| PERSONALLY IDENTIFIABLE INFORMATION (PII) | This is information that can be used on its own to locate, contact, or identify an individual. |
| PHYSICAL CONTROLS | These are physical things that can help to secure an environment. These might include fences, mantraps, fire alarms and security guards. |
| PRIVILEGE ESCALATION | Privilege escalation attacks are concerned with ways that attackers can elevate their privilege level to admin or system level permissions. |
| REVERSE ENGINEERING | Reverse engineering is the act of looking at a completed project and trying to determine how it works. This could involve taking the product apart, probing parts, or just examining it. |
| ROOTKIT | A rootkit is a collection of software tools that can help an attacker to gain access, escalate privileges, and hide their presence on a system. |
| SANDBOXING | Sandboxing is the practice of taking an application out of the network so that it can be tested. |
| SCADA | SCADA systems are used to control industrial control devices. |
| SIGNATURE ANALYSIS | Comparing the hash (signature) of one software against other software. This is often done to identify malware. |

| | |
|---|---|
| SIEM | SIEM stands for security information event manager. SIEM will take in data from a variety of places, such as syslog servers and netflow analyzers, and allow users to do data analytics on all of the data that they have received from all of these devices. |
| SOCIAL ENGINEERING | Social engineering is when an attacker will psychologically manipulate someone into divulging information or performing a desired action. |
| SYSLOG | A host based logging mechanism, and a centralized logging server. |
| TREND ANALYSIS | A system that is analyzing trends will look at current and past trends to try to predict the future. |
| TOPOLOGY | A topology is how the communication devices are laid out in the network. There are a few different topologies, including star, bus, ring, mesh, point to point, and hybrid. |
| VIRTUAL PRIVATE NETWORK (VPN) | Virtual private networks extend private networks across a public network. |
| VULNERABILITY SCANNER | A vulnerability scanner is a piece of software that scans individual hosts or networks for vulnerabilities. |
| WIRESHARK | Wireshark is a software tool that allows users to look at specific packets in a network and to organize that traffic in many different ways. |
| XSS | XSS (Cross-Site Scripting) attacks are when an attacker is able to inject, or embed, a script on a webpage that will later run on other computers that visit that website. |
| ZERO DAY | A zero day is when a previously unknown vulnerability is exploited. |

Ingram Content Group UK Ltd.
Milton Keynes UK
UKHW021610040423
419584UK00006B/52